BCA 50

Wild Australasia

Wild Australasia

Foreword by Tim Flannery

Neil Nightingale, Jeni Clevers, Hugh Pearson, Mary Summerill

BOOKS

This book is published in Australia and New Zealand to accompany the television series Wild Australasia, first broadcast in 2004.

Published by BBC Books, BBC Worldwide Ltd, Woodlands, 80 Wood Lane, London W12 0TT

First published 2003, this edition published in Australia and New Zealand in 2004

Copyright © Neil Nightingale, Jeni Clevers, Hugh Pearson, Mary Summerill

The moral right of the authors has been asserted.

ISBN 0 563 48822 0

Commissioning Editors: Shirley Patton and Nicky Ross
Project Editor: Martin Redfern
Designer: Lisa Pettibone
Copy Editor: Caroline Taggart
Picture Researcher: Frances Abraham
Cartographer: Olive Pearson
Production Controller: Kenneth McKay

Set in Gill Sans and Albertina
Printed and bound in Singapore by Tien Wah Press
Colour separations by Radstock Reproductions Limited, Midsomer Norton

Contents

4 OCEANS
Hugh Pearson   **116**

The northern part of Australia reaches into the tropics; to the south it faces Antarctica. The seas that surround it reflect this diversity, from the muddy waters in the north, with their ferocious tides, to the raging Southern Ocean, the wildest place on the planet. In between lie two of the world's most magnificent coral reefs, the world-famous Great Barrier Reef and the less famous but idyllic Ningaloo Reef. These seas are home to sharks and dugongs, sea horses and angelfish, as well as the hardest-working sea lions in the world.

5 ISLANDS
Neil Nightingale   **152**

From tropical paradise to fiery volcano or bleak windswept rock, the islands that surround Australia are as diverse as the country itself. Nearest is New Guinea, a volatile adolescent compared with the geologically stable Australia, and home to the magical birds of paradise. Further away and calmer is Lord Howe Island, a Pacific idyll where sooty terns and spectacular tropic birds breed. The oldest and strangest of all are New Caledonia, so named because it reminded Captain Cook of Scotland, and New Zealand, where the flightless kiwi behaves like a hedgehog and the world's slowest-breeding parrot may yet manage to survive.

6 NEW WORLDS
Mary Summerill   **190**

Australia's wildlife had thousands of generations in which to establish a rapport with the Aborigines before European settlers arrived and decided they wanted to make the country more like home. The introduction of European species such as the rabbit and the fox quickly upset the delicate natural balance and more recent introductions, such as the cane toad, have also got seriously out of hand. But in remote corners and offshore islands, species that were previously unknown or were thought extinct are still being discovered, and endangered species hang on to life.

Foreword

In 1770, Captain James Cook's *Endeavour* sailed up Australia's east coast, landing at various places so that Sir Joseph Banks could collect botanical and other specimens. On returning to England the expedition brought news of a vast region of the globe – a fifth part of the world – previously knows as *terra incognita*. Of all the curiosities brought back, the animals and plants created the greatest sensation. News of that remarkable creature the kangaroo spread through the streets of London like wildfire, as members of learned societies pondered the nature of such novel plants as the eucalypt and banksia.

That first glimpse of life on the Great South Land proved so intriguing that it triggered a series of scientific expeditions, and within 40 years all the major powers of Europe had sent vessels filled with scientists and artists to bring back specimens of Australian natural history. Many of their discoveries were extraordinary. Indeed some – such the egg-laying, duck-billed platypus – were scarcely to be believed. It would take scientists more than 150 years to discover just why Australia's plants and animals are so different. The revolutionary theory of continental drift finally supplied the answer: it revealed that Australia had been isolated from the other continents for 45 million years, and that over this unimaginably long time its creatures and plants had evolved in isolation. By contrast, the Americas and Eurasia have been isolated for 'only' 10,000 years – less than one four-thousandth as long as Australia. So different had Australian life become during its long period of isolation that the discoveries made by those pioneers of natural science came as close as any Earth-bound biologist will ever come to encountering life from another planet.

Australia is the size of Europe, extending from the tropics deep into the temperate regions, and including deserts, tropical rainforests, snowfields, tall hardwood forests and wetlands. But despite its size and variety, those great determinants of life – soils and climate – share a commonality across the continent. They are also unique, meaning that in Australia evolution proceeds to the beat of a very different drum from other continents.

Australia is an ancient land, having experienced little recent mountain building, volcanic activity or glacial action. This makes its soils infertile and thin. And its climate is dominated by El Niño to a greater extent than any other landmass. This means that Australia is truly, as a famous poem goes, a land of drought and flooding rain, where life pulses not to seasonal change, but to the vagaries of the world's least predictable pattern of rain. Yet somehow this impoverished, unpredictable land supports colossal biodiversity, with more than twice the number of species found in Europe and the U.S. combined. When you add to that diversity the extraordinary richness of the Australasian islands, such as New Guinea, New Caledonia and New Zealand, you have what is arguably the most intriguing natural realm on Earth.

Australia's creatures don't come much more bizarre than this thorny devil.

For all its difference, Australian nature has sometimes produced superficially similar results to those seen on other continents. The gliding possum looks remarkably like a squirrel; the marsupial mole closely resembles an African golden mole. Yet when it comes to the details of their life, wonders of contrast and complexity emerge. Australasia is a region of subtlety, diversity, and above all the unexpected. Its spirit has been beautifully captured in *Wild Australasia*. This book is as perfect an introduction as one could wish to the natural riches of this fifth part of the world.

Professor Tim Flannery
Director, South Australian Museum

Introduction

Even at first glance, Australia looks different from all the other continents. Nowhere else on Earth can you watch big red kangaroos bounding through the dunes of a red desert. The wildlife here is an astonishing mix of the strange and deadly, with more unique species than anywhere else – 90 per cent of its reptiles and 70 per cent of its birds are found only in Australia and where else do you find wombats or wallabies, kookaburras or koalas? Here there are mammals that lay eggs, huge birds that can't fly, marsupials that can, and a greater concentration of big, predatory reptiles and venomous snakes than anywhere on the planet. The land, too, looks remarkably different: a parched, sunburnt country, at times its colours mute and faded but often also glowing, with deep red rocks set against vast blue skies. This is the flattest and driest inhabited continent on Earth, with some of the oldest rocks and spectacular, time-worn landscapes. Much of Australia even smells distinctive, because it is dominated by one type of tree, the eucalypt, whose volatile oils give off an unmistakable odour that pervades both countryside and city.

But why is Australia so unusual? To understand that you have to travel back in time.

ISLAND CONTINENT

To put it at its simplest, the animals and plants are unique because Australia is an island and has been so for an almost unimaginable period of time. But the origins of much of the wildlife can be traced back even further to a period over 100 million years ago when Australia was attached to Africa, South America, India and Antarctica in the great supercontinent of Gondwana. You can still get a feel for that ancient period today simply by stepping into an Australian rainforest. These magical, tangled worlds have a timeless air and many of the plants are similar to those that grew in the Gondwanan forests – tree ferns, southern beech, cycads, palms and the luxuriant blossoms of primitive flowering plants. The rainforests are bursting with animals and many of these – the marsupials, parrots, platypus and large flightless birds – also had ancestors on that ancient supercontinent.

However, the most significant event in Australian natural history was yet to come – massive forces within the Earth slowly broke Gondwana apart. That split took an enormous length of time but eventually, about 45 million years ago, Australia severed its final connections with the rest of the world. From then on it would never again be joined to any other land and so its cargo of wildlife was able to evolve alone, largely free from the competition of species from elsewhere. In their isolation, the animals and plants adapted to the specific conditions of this island continent, evolving in unique and often strange ways.

Nowhere provides a better glimpse of that ancient world and the spectacular diversity of early Australian wildlife than a remote fossil site at Riversleigh in Queensland. The extraordinary finds here date back about 25 million years and are some of the most extensive fossil remains anywhere on Earth. Today

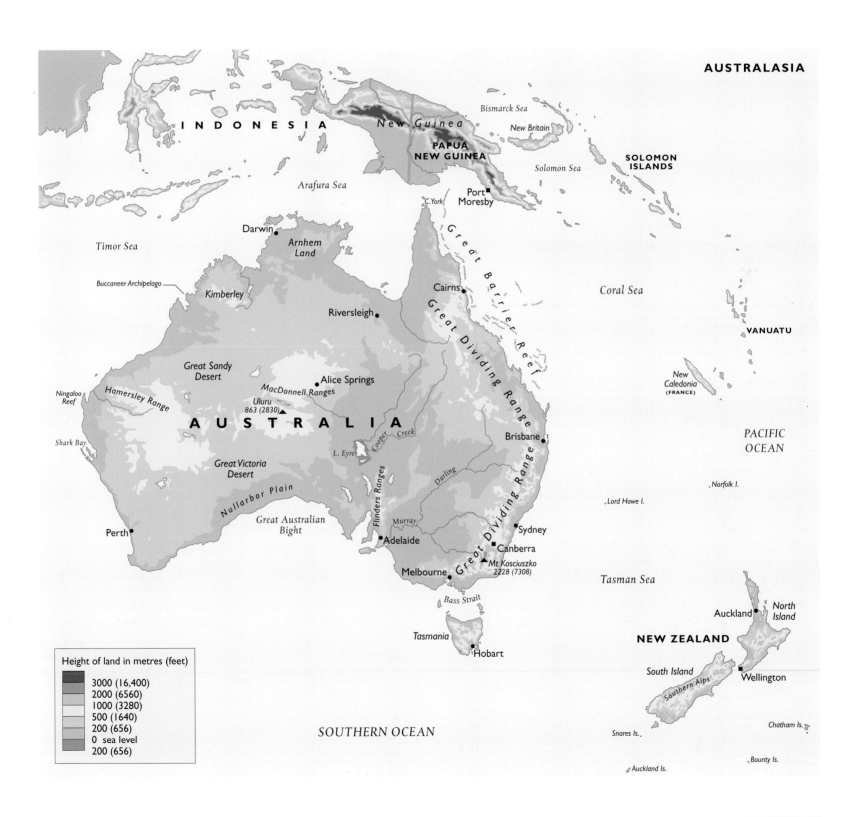

AUSTRALASIA

INDONESIA

Bismarck Sea

New Guinea

PAPUA NEW GUINEA

New Britain

SOLOMON ISLANDS

Solomon Sea

Arafura Sea

C.York

Port Moresby

Coral Sea

Timor Sea

Darwin

Arnhem Land

Buccaneer Archipelago

Kimberley

Cairns

Great Barrier Reef

VANUATU

Riversleigh

New Caledonia (FRANCE)

Great Sandy Desert

Alice Springs

Great Dividing Range

Ningaloo Reef

Hamersley Range

MacDonnell Ranges

Uluru 863 (2830) ▲

AUSTRALIA

PACIFIC OCEAN

Shark Bay

Cooper Creek

Brisbane

Norfolk I.

Great Victoria Desert

L. Eyre

Darling

Great Dividing Range

Lord Howe I.

Nullarbor Plain

Flinders Ranges

Murray

Sydney

Perth

Great Australian Bight

Adelaide

Canberra ▲ *Mt Kosciuszko* 2228 (7308)

Melbourne

Tasman Sea

Bass Strait

Auckland

North Island

Tasmania

NEW ZEALAND

Hobart

South Island

Southern Alps

Wellington

Height of land in metres (feet)

	3000 (16,400)
	2000 (6560)
	1000 (3280)
	500 (1640)
	200 (656)
	0 sea level
	200 (656)

SOUTHERN OCEAN

Snares Is.

Chatham Is.

Auckland Is.

Bounty Is.

1

Riversleigh is a parched and rocky landscape, so it's hard to imagine that back then it was covered in thick forests, swamps and lakes which teemed with giant crocodiles and turtles, large platypus, huge flightless birds, a whole variety of possums and lumbering marsupial herbivores, some with trunks like modern tapirs. A great range of hunters roamed the forests – wolf-like thylacines, marsupial lions, even carnivorous kangaroos. It was a unique mixture of the familiar and the bizarre. Over 150 different collections of fossils from various distinct ages have been found at Riversleigh and they reveal that this location, like much of Australia, remained green and well vegetated until roughly 15 million years ago.

But the good times could not last for ever. Complex changes in the world's ocean currents and winds altered the global climate and Australia gradually began to dry out. Rainforests retreated to a few moist corners and were replaced by open forest, woodland, scrub and grassland – the typical Aussie bush. Some rainforest plants, such as acacias, casuarinas and banksias, evolved to cope superbly with this new world and one group in particular now dominates much of it – the eucalypts or gums. There are over 700 species and 99 per cent of them live naturally only in Australia. From stately river red to woolybutt, ghost gum to coolibah, these trees are as distinctly Australian as the kangaroo, koala and kookaburra.

Not surprisingly, the overall drying had a dramatic effect on Australia's rivers – some simply dried up. Today, parts of the interior are below sea level, so many rivers flow inland rather than towards the coast and their water eventually evaporates in the burning heat of the centre. The largest river system on the continent, the Murray–Darling, which drains one-seventh of Australia's surface, has an annual flow that is less than a single day of the Amazon's. Most of the time it is just a series of billabongs and sluggish channels. Even if you added up the water in all Australia's rivers, their combined annual flow would still be less than half that of the Mississippi. Only the frozen wastes of Antarctica contain less running water than Australia – this really is an incredibly parched place.

In the last few million years the drying intensified until today two-thirds of Australia is arid and almost half is actually desert – from the huge rolling sand dunes of the Simpson in the east to the endless spinifex grasslands of the Tanami in the north, and from the vast stony plains of the Gibson in Western Australia to the beautiful carved mountains of the Red Centre. If lack of rainfall were not bad enough, the climate is also famously unpredictable. One part of the desert may have no rain at all for years, then suddenly drown in torrential floods. It's a tricky place to live, but these fickle conditions have produced a unique range of wildlife able to cope – animals don't come much

1. Ironically for such a dry continent, much of the landscape has been shaped by water, like this deep gorge at Karijini National Park, Western Australia.

Overleaf: Gum trees feature prominently in landscapes right across the continent, like this desert scene at Haasts Bluff in the Northern Territories.

tougher than a piratical monitor lizard, a gang of inventive galahs or an emu whose legs can stride all day in search of a drop of water. The largest of all marsupials, the red kangaroo, has the ability to survive off the most meagre rations and yet breed at a moment's notice when food and water allow. At the other end of the scale, miniature termites exist in prodigious numbers, eating more vegetation than all the other animals combined and surviving the oppressive heat in giant air-conditioned mounds and underground chambers.

Since it broke away, this island ark has been drifting north across the globe at the stately pace of 6–7 cm (2–3 inches) a year but, apart from that gentle drift, it has been in something of a geological slumber; there has been little volcanic activity or mountain building. The mainland of Australia has only two major mountain ranges, the MacDonnells in the centre and the Great Dividing Range down the east coast, and both are puny by world stan-dards. The highest point, Mount Kosciuszko, is just 2228 m (7308 feet) above sea level. Instead, the forces of wind and water have, over huge periods of time, worked to wear Australia down until now it's the flattest of all continents. Such a long period of erosion has also worn out most of the soils, so the animals and plants have to endure some of the world's thinnest, most fragile and least productive land.

As Australia slowly drifted north, its leading edge eventually entered the tropics, which means that today the far north not only feels the influence of the nearby desert but also gets hit by one of the most powerful climate systems on the planet, the Asian monsoon. Many months of the year remain tinder dry and the tropical savannah regularly bursts into flames. However, when the monsoon descends, the same land is subject to torrential rain, violent tropical storms and cyclones. Ironically, this brutal regime has created some of the most starkly beautiful regions of all – the Top End, Kimberley and Cape York, which stretch right across the top of the continent. Here you'll find exquisitely sculpted rock formations, spectacular waterfalls and some of the world's largest tropical swamps, home to giant crocodiles and immense flocks of water birds.

As this isolated world edged closer to Asia, new animal groups, such as rats and mice, and more species of bats, birds and reptiles found their way across the narrowing sea. But the most significant migrants were yet to arrive. About 60,000 years ago Australia was discov-ered and settled by humans. Their descendants, the Aborigines, may represent the oldest continuous culture on Earth. The harsh climate, poor soils and thin vegetation limited popula-tions so that they never grew to the density of other continents, but their numbers may have been sufficient to contribute to the extinction of many large marsupials. People also altered the ecology of much of the continent with their extensive use of fire to manage the vegetation and help them with hunting.

After humans arrived there was still one major global event that was to change the shape of the continent completely. At the end of the Ice Age, about 8000 years ago, melting glaciers caused world sea levels to rise by over 100 m (330 feet). New Guinea and Tasmania, which until then had been connected to the mainland, were cut off as islands. Around its edge about 15 per cent of Australia was drowned by the rising seas, creating its dramatic modern coastline. In the far north-west, river valleys were flooded to create the beautiful Buccaneer Archipelago, a stunning mosaic of islands and long peninsulas in an azure sea. A similar process created a vast natural harbour, in fact the world's largest, around which modern Sydney is built. And off the east coast, as the edge of the continental shelf sank under water, the Great Barrier Reef grew into its modern form. Today over 4000 separate reefs and islands stretching over 2300 km (1500 miles) of ocean make this by far the largest living structure on the planet.

Very early in Australia's history New Zealand and New Caledonia broke away from the mainland and these islands have since evolved their own unique, but related, animals and plants. As Australia has drifted north many volcanic and other islands (such as New Guinea, New Britain and Lord Howe) have also been pushed up out of the sea along the fringes of its continental plate. These islands stretch from the equator down into the sub-Antarctic and form the larger region called Australasia.

The result of this epic natural history is a dry, crusty old continent rimmed with rainforest and reef and with seas dotted with a fabulous string of islands. In both Australia and the islands, long periods of isolation and particular environmental conditions have created just about the most surprising combination of animals, plants and landscapes on Earth.

RAINFORESTS

TROPICAL RAINFORESTS

Previous page:
The tropical rain-
forests of Australia
are complex, three-
dimensional worlds
and home to a vast
variety of plant species.

Australia was once a lush, green continent and thick forests were common. Today things could not be more different. It's now so parched and rainfall so unreliable that forests have retreated to just a few corners and the activities of European settlers in the last 200 years have pushed them back even further. The most luxuriant vegetation of all is tropical rainforest and today it grows on just a tiny fraction of the continent, in the far northeast. Here it clings to the slopes of a few coastal mountains, where sufficient rainfall and relatively inaccessible locations have allowed it to survive. In spite of its small extent, it brims over with wildlife, supporting more animal and plant species than any other environment in Australia. It also represents a very ancient community. Rainforests grew here at least 100 million years ago, long before Australia became an island. If you had to pick the most important wildlife habitat in all Australia, this would certainly be it.

JUNGLE BY THE SEA

Just a short drive north of Cairns in Queensland, a chain-driven car ferry takes you across the gentle waters of the Daintree River and into another world. Rainforest-clad mountains rise from the deep blue of the Coral Sea. Along the coast long sandy beaches alternate with rocky headlands, mangroves and swamp forests. Take just a short stroll from the road, along any of the frequent boardwalks, and it is like stepping back in time. The towering forest trees cut out much of the light, while climbing vines seem to smother every bare trunk in their race for the sun. On the higher branches, orchids, mosses, lichens and ferns of all shapes and textures perch like miniature gardens in the sky. In the shade of the forest floor, ancient cycads and king ferns sprout. In damper areas, exquisite stands of fan palms glow in the rare and constantly shifting shafts of sunlight. Lowland tropical rainforest such as this is the most luxuriant habitat on the continent and the Daintree region contains the largest remaining area in all Australia.

As well as feeling ancient, the rainforests of the wet tropics have several claims actually to be so. For a start they contain many plants whose large, simple flowers are very similar to fossils of the earliest flowers ever to exist. One particular vine called Austrobaileya has pollen that is virtually identical to fossil pollen from 110 million years ago, close to the time when the very first flowers appeared on Earth. There are 19 families of such primitive flowers known worldwide and Daintree has representatives of 13 of them. One of the reasons these particular forests contain such species is that rainforests have existed here constantly for such an enormous length of time. They may have shrunk or expanded as the climate and landscape changed, but they never completely disappeared.

Part of the key to that survival has been the mountainous nature of this coast. At times, when the lowlands dried out, forest was able to hang on higher up, often in deep gorges. Today the wild slopes, high plateaus and steep valleys contain almost every type of tropical rainforest, growing on a whole variety of rocks and soils. Some slopes face east and are regularly ravaged by tropical cyclones, while others are more sheltered and support massively tall trees, adding further to the diversity of the forest.

The largest section of Australian tropical rainforest stretches in a narrow band down the coast from Cooktown in the north to near Townsville 450 km (300 miles) further south, with Daintree and Mounts Bartle Frere and Bellenden Kerr at its heart. These are the highest mountains in the area, rising over 1500 m (4900 feet) from the sea, catching the moist winds off the Pacific and generating their own clouds and climate. Here it can rain over 10 m (33 feet) a year. As a lush, green

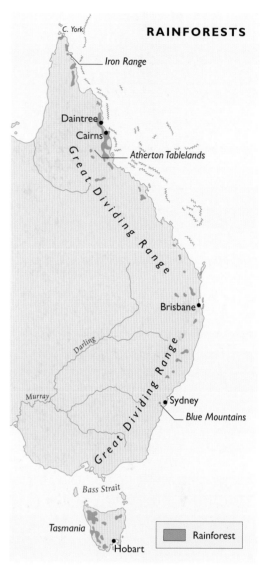

RAINFORESTS

1. Near Cape Tribulation, in the Daintree area of Queensland, rainforest grows right down to the sea.

fringe to a largely dry, brown continent, this forest and its surrounding habitats are of enormous natural value – a fact that was recognized in 1988 when the Queensland Wet Tropics were listed as a World Heritage Area. Covering just one-thousandth of Australia's land surface, this protected area remarkably supports about 25 per cent of all Australia's reptile and amphibian species, 30 per cent of the marsupials, 50 per cent of the birds and almost 60 per cent of the different bats and butterflies. Over 3000 species of plants also grow here and almost a quarter are found nowhere else.

Plant power

In a place like this you simply cannot ignore the plants. They are in control, determining where you can and cannot go, and it's not just the general tangle that makes progress difficult. Appropriately named 'wait-a-while' vines use hooks to help them climb towards the sun and their barbed shoots seem to hang at ankle, arm and head height throughout the forest. To be caught brings you to an instant and painful halt, but that is a mild inconvenience compared with the excruciating pain inflicted by stinging trees, which often grow on disturbed ground at the side of paths. The stinging hairs are as sharp as glass and contain a potent mixture of acids and other chemicals which cause severe blistering pain that lasts for several hours and can recur for weeks or even months.

Perhaps the most sinister plant of the forest, although harmless to us, is the strangler fig. Its seeds are carried and then dropped by birds and they germinate on branches in the canopy. Initially they depend on the detritus trapped up there to fertilize their growth, but at a certain size they send down roots all the way to the ground to tap into the nutrients on the forest floor. These aerial roots thicken, new ones grow and eventually they strangle the trunk of their host tree with a network of stout fibres. The strangler's leaves also shade its host and, as the years pass, the original tree dies and rots away, often leaving a hollow lattice work of strangler roots. There is a fabulous example of this less than a metre (3 feet) off the path at the Marrdja boardwalk in Daintree National Park.

At Yungaburra on the Atherton Tablelands, little more than an hour's drive away, the curtain strangler fig is one of the wonders of the botanical world. The tree that it was strangling was so weakened that it fell over against another, so that it was leaning at an angle. The strangler then sent down more roots along the entire length of the trunk to create a massive cascade that tumbles to the ground like a gigantic, fancy curtain. Looking up at this monster it is hard to imagine a more telling example of the sheer power and dominance of plant life in these ideal conditions for growth.

 ## BUMPY SATIN ASH

The flowers of many rainforest trees are hard to spot high in the canopy, but not those of the bumpy satin ash, which sprout in large, creamy clusters directly from the trunk, from ground level upwards. This habit is called cauliflory and biologists believe it evolved to help these trees attract bird and mammal pollinators, which find it easier to use the firm trunk as a base for feeding rather than dangling from branch tips in the canopy. The concentrated supply of nectar delivered at such an easy height makes blooming bumpy satin ashes great places for wildlife-watching. During the day honey-eaters, lorikeets, bees and other insects fly in to dine. At night bats, moths and possums are the main customers. One animal frequently attracted to the feast is the long-tailed pygmy possum, a diminutive creature just 10 cm (4 inches) long. With such a small body size it has to feed almost continuously and a trunk full of flowers is a real bonus. Striped possums (left), which normally hunt for beetle grubs, also find the blooms irresistible. Usually just one or two blossoms from a bunch open each night and so the flowering continues for up to two months.

1. The curtain fig is so called because of its mass of aerial roots, which cascade down like a curtain.

2. Beautiful fan palms are characteristic of lowland rainforests, especially in areas where the soil is permanently moist.

Each year a single hectare (2 ½ acres) of tropical rainforest can produce 10 tonnes of fallen branches and leaf litter for decomposers to work on.

Feast for the birds

The plants may dominate in the rainforests, but they need partners if they are to survive, especially when it comes to dispersing their seeds. Many employ birds as couriers, attracting them with a rich feast of succulent fruits. So fruiting trees are one of the best places in the forest for bird-watching.

Pigeons and fruit doves are some of the most beautiful visitors and the wompoo fruit dove is one of the easiest to spot – large and colourful with a distinctive call. Many pigeons fly great distances over the forest, which makes them excellent seed carriers. The Torresian imperial pigeon migrates between New Guinea and Australia and even when in Australia tends to migrate daily, feeding in coastal rainforest and then flying to roost in the relative safety of offshore islands. At the right time of year you can watch flocks of dozens and sometimes hundreds of these distinctive black and white birds departing at sunset and flying out over the sea.

Parrots are also attracted to fruits, although they will often destroy the seeds inside rather than dispersing them. The daintiest of all are the double-eyed fig parrots, Australia's smallest parrots. Emerald green with a blue and red face, they nest in decaying trees and feed mainly on cluster figs. Eclectus parrots, which live only in the rainforests of Cape York, are unusual in that males and females look strikingly different. The males are green and the females bright red. Nobody knows why, but it was so confusing that for a long time they were classified as separate species. Perhaps the most vibrant of all parrots are the rainbow lorikeets. These are specialist nectar- and pollen-feeders, with long, brush-like tongues to reach inside flowers. By unwittingly transferring pollen between blooms they help to pollinate the flowers. Their multi-coloured plumage, noisy calls and habit of hurtling round in large flocks make them some of the most conspicuous of all the forest birds.

1. (opposite) Rainbow lorikeets have specialized brush-like tongues for licking up nectar, and a simple gut to cope with this liquid diet.

Overleaf: The male and female eclectus parrot are strikingly different in colour, so much so that they were once thought to be different species.

 CASSOWARY–TYRANT OR GENTLE GIANT?

Standing as tall as a person, the flightless cassowary (left) is far and away the most impressive bird in the rainforest. With spiky black feathers, startling blue skin on its face and neck, bright red throat wattles and a horny casque rather like a crash helmet perched on its head, this is a bizarre-looking bird. It is formidable, too, with strong legs that can deliver a powerful kick, made even more dangerous by the rapier-like toe-nails on each foot. And it has an attitude to match its weaponry. If a cassowary is cornered it will charge and a single kick from those sharp toes can easily slash open a deep wound. They are no more considerate towards each other, preferring to remain solitary, and threatening and chasing off strangers. But there is a soft side to the males. When the eggs are laid, the female is free to seek another mate and it is the male that incubates them for about seven weeks, hardly leaving the nest to eat or drink during that entire time. He will then care tenderly for the chicks for up to a year, sheltering them under his feathers, teaching them what to eat and even breaking large fruits into bite-sized lumps. At all times the male is alert to danger and will chase off predators as large as goannas, dingoes, and even people. But all this tender paternal care has to come to an end at some stage. Abruptly, when the chicks are about a year old, their father reverts to type, becomes aggressive towards his youngsters and chases them off into the forest.

★ The highest annual rainfall recorded in Australia was 11,251 mm (over 440 inches), which fell on Mount Bellenden Kerr in 1979.

1

2

Insects everywhere

With so many plants to eat you would think a rainforest would be teeming with wildlife, but at first glance this is not obvious. Partly that's because the most numerous animals are small – the insects and other creepy-crawlies. There are so many species that the total is simply not known. They are everywhere and perform many important functions in the forest. Wood-boring beetles, termites and cockroaches break down fallen timber on the forest floor; butterflies, bees and flies pollinate flowers in the canopy; caterpillars, katydids, stick insects and other herbivores eat more vegetation than all the larger animals combined, while a whole range of hunters – spiders, preying mantids and predatory ants – set traps for the unwary.

In the depths of the forest you have to look hard to spot these smaller creatures, but forest clearings, where the sun streams in, provide easier opportunities. If climbing vines or other flowers have bloomed in the sunlight, you stand a good chance of seeing some of the rainforest's stunningly beautiful butterflies. Their names alone provide some idea of the aerial acrobatics to expect: skipper, cruiser, lurcher, birdwing, moon-beam, even aeroplane. The most magnificent of all is surely the Cairns birdwing, Australia's largest butterfly, which cruises slowly through the canopy or hovers by a flower on enormous black and gold wings 20 cm (8 inches) across. But in the glamour stakes another species can justifiably claim to be even more spectacular – the Ulysses. It is not quite as large as the birdwing, but its upper wings are a brilliant and iridescent metallic blue and that colour flashes on and off with each wing beat, creating a dazzling aerial display.

1. In contrast to the bright colour on top, the under-wings of the Ulysses butterfly are dark, so when it flies the iridescent blue appears to flash on and off.

2. The birdwings are amongst the largest and most spectacular of all the rainforest butterflies.

 MUSKY RAT KANGAROO

During the day most marsupials are fast asleep, but not the musky rat kangaroo (right). It is the smallest and most primitive member of the kangaroo and wallaby family and lives only in tropical rainforest. Kangaroos originally evolved from possum-like ancestors and in many ways the musky rat kangaroo represents an intermediate form. Like possums, it retains a 'big toe' on its hind feet which helps it scramble over fallen trees and branches and, although it has long back legs, it prefers to gallop on all fours rather than hop. Its diet is also very unlike that of other kangaroos. It forages in the leaf litter for fallen fruit, insects, earthworms and other invertebrates, often hoarding the fruit and also dispersing the seeds of rainforest trees. At night and during the hottest part of the day it rests in a nest of dried leaves, usually in the seclusion of a clump of vines. It has a very curious way of collecting this nesting material, first picking the leaves up with its forepaws, transferring them to its hind feet and then kicking them into its back-curved tail which wraps around the leaves and carries them to the nest.

The striped possum has the largest brain of any marsupial relative to body size, perhaps the result of having to forage in the complex three-dimensional world of the rainforest.

Hidden hunters

Many of the larger forest animals are not immediately obvious because they are well camouflaged. Reptiles thrive in the tropical heat and there are lots of them here, including snakes. Fortunately most rainforest species are harmless to humans, so even if you pass inadvertently close you are unlikely to be attacked. They range in size from small burrowing snakes, just 20 cm (8 inches) long, to the amethystine python, Australia's largest and a rainforest specialist. The record for a amethystine python is over 8 m (26 feet), although most are more like half this length, but that's still big enough to catch a small wallaby. They hunt mainly at night using special heat receptors in their jaws to detect their prey, even in complete darkness. During the day their motionless form is easy to overlook amongst leaf litter or on a branch .

Lizards, too, are common, but even the most spectacular species, Boyd's forest dragon, can be difficult to spot. It hunts for insects and other invertebrates, but much of the time remains motionless, perched on a branch. Although it has a dramatic crest of pointed scales, a conspicuous yellow and white face and bright yellow chin pouch, in the dappled light of the forest understorey it is effectively camouflaged and can be surprisingly easy to miss.

Rainforest geckos also rely on superbly cryptic camouflage to avoid detection while resting during the day. The northern leaf-tailed gecko is the most curious-looking of all, with the colour and pattern of bark and numerous small spines to break up its outline. It also sports an extraordinary large, flat, leaf-shaped tail, which it raises and waves when disturbed. The tail is larger than its head and probably acts as a decoy for predators such as owls and snakes. When the gecko is attacked, the tail simply drops off. The gecko escapes and later grows a new tail which, unlike the original, does not have spikes.

3

Forest nights

As the sun sets the rainforest takes on a whole new perspective. Numerous animals wake up, including possums which spend the day sleeping high in the forks of branches or deep inside hollow trees. The Queensland rainforest contains several specialized possums that live nowhere else, including four species of ringtails: the green, lemuroid, Daintree River and Herbert River ringtails. They live only in mountain forests, feed mostly on leaves and use their prehensile tails as a fifth limb to help them move through the canopy. Most climb slowly and deliberately, but the lemuroid is more agile than the others and leaps from branch to branch, more like a lemur than a possum, hence its name.

The boldly marked striped possum is far more active than the leaf-eaters, scrambling noisily through the forest, up in the canopy and down on the forest floor, searching for wood-boring grubs. When it detects one

4

1. Dragon lizards are common throughout Australia and Boyd's forest dragon is a rainforest specialist.

2. The remarkable-looking leaf-tailed gecko is so well camouflaged it is almost invisible against the bark of a tree.

3. The amethystine python hangs in wait for warm-blooded mammals and birds which it senses with special heat detectors in its jaws.

4. The fur of the lemuroid ringtail possum is usually grey but a few individuals in the Mount Carbine region are a striking cream colour.

beneath the surface of a log or rotten branch it uses its long incisors to break away the bark and then winkles out the juicy grub with a specially elongated finger.

Often the only regular sound at night is the soft hum of insects, but during the wet season the night comes alive with noise; the massed calls of breeding frogs – chirps, chuckles, trills, whistles, purrs and croaks – come from all directions. The frogs are incredibly varied, from the tiny litter frogs just a centimetre or so (1/2 inch) long to the giant tree frog, which can grow as large as a dinner plate and is Australia's biggest. Some inhabit the canopy, others burrow beneath the forest floor; they live inside rotting wood, beside streams and under waterfalls – in fact almost everywhere in the rainforest.

Their breeding behaviour is as varied as the rest of their biology. Most lay eggs in water, but nursery frogs and whistling frogs take advantage of the protection and moist conditions under the leaf litter and deposit their eggs there. These hatch, not into tadpoles, but directly into baby froglets. Even stranger are the two species of gastric brooders. In these species the mother swallows the eggs, which then hatch inside her. The tadpoles are protected in the stomach for several weeks until finally they metamorphose into froglets and emerge from her mouth. During this time the mother's stomach swells to an enormous size – not surprising with over 20 large tadpoles inside. But how do they avoid being digested by stomach acids? It seems that both eggs and tadpoles secrete a chemical that turns off their mother's stomach secretions during her unusual 'pregnancy'. There are still many mysteries surrounding these gastric brooders and research is limited because the frogs are so rare. In fact neither species has been seen for many years and they may already be extinct.

The gastric brooders are not the only recent discoveries in Australia's rainforests. This area is so rich in life and yet so relatively little studied that new species come to light every year. Half of all rainforest frogs, for example, have been described since 1970 and many of these new species have small populations, some declining fast. This relatively small corner of Australia may have by far the greatest diversity of wildlife on the continent but at the same time it is very fragile, making it an exceptionally precious place.

1. (opposite) The common green tree frog lives in almost every habitat in the Australian tropics, even in people's homes.

WOLLEMI PINE

The Blue Mountains rise on the outskirts of Sydney, less than 100 km (60 miles) from the Harbour Bridge. They are a vast wilderness of peaks, crags and sandstone cliffs with a maze of hundreds of deep canyons. The forested slopes are covered mainly in eucalypt but in the canyons, protected from bushfires and drought, pockets of lush temperate rainforest grow. One day in September 1994, in one of these canyons, a bushwalker made a remarkable discovery, finding a tree that had been previously known only from fossils and which had been thought to be extinct for millions of years. Later searches revealed fewer than 40 adult trees, making this one of the rarest plants on the planet. Named the Wollemi pine after the Wollemi wilderness area where it lives, it is a type of monkey puzzle that grows to 40 m (130 feet) high and has a very unusual and distinctive knobbly bark (left). Pollen identical to that of the Wollemi pine is known in fossil form from about 100 million years ago, so it seems these remarkable trees have been around for longer than the island of Australia itself.

COOL RAINFORESTS

As you travel south, tropical turns to subtropical rainforest, which looks superficially similar but generally has fewer species of animals and plants. Further south this in turn is replaced by temperate rainforest, which has its own distinct collection of wildlife and a very different feel – cool and clammy, with just a few dominant types of tree and a clearer understorey. But what these forests lack in diversity they more than make up with a mystical, mist-shrouded character. Like the tropical rainforests to the north they are ancient reminders of forests that grew on the supercontinent of Gondwana 100 million years ago.

Such rainforests were once common on the slopes of the Great Dividing Range in both New South Wales and Victoria, but logging of valuable timber has reduced them to tiny, isolated fragments. Today Australia's only extensive areas grow on the cool, wet island of Tasmania: some of the most important temperate rainforests on Earth.

TASMANIAN RAINFOREST

Tasmania is a rugged, mountainous island lying in the path of the 'roaring forties', the moist winds that howl in from the Southern Ocean and rise up over the coastal mountains to create cloud, mist, snow and torrential rain. This regular rainfall, and Tasmania's position at the southern tip of the continent, gives it a feel that is perhaps the least typically Australian of any part of the country. At times it's easy to imagine you are in Europe or North America. This unique geography allows extensive areas of cool temperate rainforest to grow and even today it still covers over 10 per cent of the island.

The mountains not only encourage a wet climate, they have also provided the rainforest with considerable protection from people. The rugged landscapes of western Tasmania, with steep slopes, raging rivers, precipitous crags and a wild coastline, have largely prevented this region from being exploited in a major way. Since the British first settled Australia it has been known as a hell hole. During the early days the most desperate and dangerous convicts were sent to western Tasmania because it was a place from which it was almost impossible to escape, and many men died while trying. Of course attitudes have changed since then, but only relatively recently have the wonderful natural values of this region been truly recognized. After a high-profile environmental campaign against building dams for power generation in the 1980s, much of the rainforest has now been listed in the Tasmanian Wilderness World Heritage Area, one of the largest and most significant protected areas of this forest type on Earth.

1. The ice-carved cliffs of Cradle Mountain, Tasmania, reflected in the waters of Dove Lake.

1

Cathedrals of green

To enter these forests is to experience a quiet and subtle grandeur. At first they often feel dark, silent and still; there is not the exuberance and colour of the tropics. The most common tree is the myrtle beech and its small leaves form a dense canopy, shading out most other plants. But take time to adjust to the darkness and you'll notice that the interior glows with a soft green. Ferns of all sizes and shapes sprout everywhere, mosses and liver-worts cover fallen trees and living trunks, lichens clothe branches, rocks and any other unoccupied surfaces. The whole forest seems smothered in a soft, living carpet. Where streams, tree falls or landslides open up the canopy, other trees get a foothold – leather-woods, sassafras, blackwood and huon pines. Giant heath plants called pandani and ancient tree ferns give the place an exotic and primitive feel, but you have to search hard to find any flowers. The trees themselves have relatively small and inconspicuous blooms in green, yellow or white, as they are mostly insect- or wind-pollinated and have no need to attract bird pollinators with bright colours.

Mature forests like these take over 300 years to become established and during that time the climate has to remain constantly moist and free of bushfires, otherwise more drought- and fire-tolerant trees such as eucalypts invade. Some individual trees are truly ancient. Huon pines are magnificent, slow-growing and can live for 3000 years,

1. Tree ferns are characteristic of the moist temperate rainforests of Tasmania.

Their fine-grained wood is strong and workable, resistant to rot and ideal for boat building. It was for these valuable trees that early settlers ventured into the rainforests, but fortunately the sheer inaccessibility of the region prevented full-scale logging and allowed the wilderness to survive to this day.

Mountain and rivers

From the Arthur Range in the far south, the mountains of Tasmania curve up through the western half of the island, creating some of the most rugged land in all Australia. It is these mountains, rising up in the face of moist westerly winds, that are vital to create the rainfall so necessary for rainforest growth. Many rise well over 1000 m (3300 feet) and their rocky peaks are frequently snow-covered in winter. But not far below the bleak summits, sheltered valleys support stunted and twisted rainforests of myrtle, king billy and celery-top pine. Here it is almost permanently wet. Around one of Tasmania's most famous peaks, Cradle Mountain, rain falls about 240 days a year and the forests are more often than not clothed in mist. Swollen streams and waterfalls cascade down steep, forested gullies, and the vegetation drips into the saturated air. Almost every tree is smothered in mosses and lichens. Fallen trees decay slowly and the forest floor is a tangle of dead and decaying logs. These are magical worlds to explore.

These temperate rainforests exist alongside a range of other vegetation types which vary

depending on altitude, shelter, fire history and drainage. Where fire has taken hold at some point, woodlands of snow gum and other eucalypts alternate with open button-grass plains. At higher altitudes these plains are dotted with bright green cushion plants, enormous circular carpets of thousands of tiny flowers. Their overall shape allows them to store heat effectively, so they are perfectly suited to these cold alpine conditions. While large areas of pure rainforest may not support a great variety of animals, these mosaics positively teem with wildlife. At Cradle Mountain, the forest edge and adjacent button-grass plains are home to Bennett's wallabies, wombats, brush-tail and ringtail possums, Tasmanian devils, spotted tailed and eastern quolls, Tasmanian pademelons and echidnas. One of the most curious animals here, the freshwater crayfish, lives underground, burrowing under button grass and leaving tell-tale mounds. It is an ancient relic of Tasmania's past, with fossils dating back to Gondwanan times.

The mountains are also the start of the great rivers that tumble towards Tasmania's wild shores, carving deep valleys through the rainforests. The largest and most famous of these are the Franklin and Gordon, which eventually join to flow out into Macquarie Harbour on the west coast. In their higher reaches both rivers are powerful white-water torrents, rushing through ferocious rapids, spilling over dramatic waterfalls. In their middle sections they become navigable and the Franklin in particular is a popular rafting river. The lower reaches of the Gordon are broad and calm, winding through hills clothed in majestic lowland rainforest, the water stained a dark brown by the tannin leaching from rotting vegetation. There is no better place than the river to view this unique rain-forest whose canopy, despite its lack of species, seems to contain almost every shade of green.

2

3

1. (opposite) The Tasmanian mountains receive a covering of snow several times each winter but, except around the summits, it rarely lasts long.

2. During blizzards Bennett's wallabies take shelter at the edge of the forest or in the lee of other tall vegetation.

3. The short-beaked echidna lives in every region of Australia including Tasmania, from rainforest to desert, and feeds largely on ants, termites and beetle grubs.

⭐ Lake St Claire in Tasmania was originally carved out by glaciers during the ice ages and is now Australia's deepest lake, at almost 200 m (650 feet).

ANCIENT HUNTERS

Just as with plants, animal diversity in these cool forests is a fraction of what it is in their tropical counterparts. But Tasmanian forests have one big advantage – they are on an island. On the mainland many marsupial populations have been decimated by introduced predators such as the fox, but so far these have not got a strong foothold in Tasmania. As a result the marsupials here have been reprieved and the island contains the most complete representation of Australia's original mammal diversity found anywhere in the country.

The most famous of all the island's animals is the Tasmanian devil, extinct on the mainland for several hundred years. It inhabits rainforest and almost every other habitat, even farmland. A carrion-eater by preference, it ventures out each evening in search of dead animals, and a large wallaby carcass may attract a dozen or more devils. These animals are not generous in sharing a meal, nor are they polite, so such a scene can rapidly degenerate into noisy and apparently aggressive squabbling. Devils have powerful jaws capable of grinding bone and they charge at each other with open-mouthed screams. It's frightening to watch but, with such potentially dangerous weapons, they seem careful not to bite. Instead, if these threats don't work, they change tactics, reversing into their opponent, barging against each other with their bottoms again and again until one gives way.

It is tough being a Tasmanian devil and competition begins early in life. A mother may give birth to as many as 20 babies which all try to crawl into her pouch. They are tiny, barely larger than a human fingernail, and their sole aim is to find a nipple to latch on to. The problem is their mother has only six nipples, so competition for a position is intense and the majority of babies perish. In fact it's rare for more than four young devils from any litter to survive through to weaning. The devil is not the only carnivorous marsupial to give birth to far more young than the mother has nipples and the reason for this is still not clear.

The rainforests are also home to a smaller marsupial predator, the spotted tailed quoll.

1. The symbol of Tasmania, and the largest remaining marsupial meat-eater, is the Tasmanian devil.

2. When feeding around a carcass Tasmanian devils defend their meal with ferocious-looking threats.

3. The eastern quoll lives throughout Tasmania, hunting mainly invertebrates but also small birds and mammals.

Overleaf: Distinctive pandani plants line a winter stream.

With its fearsome claws, sharp teeth, powerful spring and spotted coat it is rather like the small hunting cats found elsewhere in the world. Incredibly agile, it uses fallen trunks as highways through the forest in its search for small birds, reptiles, mammals and invertebrates. When hunting, a mother carries the young around with her. While still suckling they hang from her belly by their mouths, which looks quite uncomfortable, but later they hitch a ride on her back.

The even smaller eastern quoll, which is now probably extinct on the mainland, completes the trio of marsupial hunters in Tasmania. These three carnivores provide a last link to the great diversity of marsupial predators that once prowled forests all over Australia.

⭐ Tasmania retains such a richness of natural wonders that almost 30 per cent of the island is protected in national parks and other reserves – more than any other state.

3

PLATYPUS – STRANGEST OF ALL MAMMALS

One Australian creature can fairly claim the prize for the strangest mammal of all. When it was first discovered by Europeans in 1799 a skin was sent back to England for analysis and identification. It seemed so improbable to the scientists of the day that they immediately declared it a hoax. That's hardly surprising when you consider that the animal in question has a bill like a duck's, fur like a mammal's, a beaver's tail, and feet that have both webs and claws. Later it was also found to be venomous, although it has no teeth. It was, of course, the duck-billed platypus and was so strange that its position in the animal kingdom confounded scientists for almost a century.

Closer investigation further heightened the mystery. Although it had fur, which is unique to mammals, its internal anatomy suggested a reproductive system closer to that of birds and reptiles. In fact, almost a century after the platypus's first discovery, it was conclusively shown that these strange creatures laid eggs, like birds. But in the meantime a number of female specimens had also been shown to have mammary glands, which secrete milk. These are the defining feature of mammals, so finally it was declared a mammal, although a very odd one indeed.

The platypus is a fairly secretive little animal and is almost impossible to breed in captivity. So the intimate details of its curious breeding habits have emerged only in the last few years and some of the precise behaviour is still a mystery. Each year a female appears to select a burrow in a stream bank, which she excavates and enlarges with the broad nails on her front feet. Within the nesting chamber she lays usually two eggs, which she then incubates for up to 10 days by curling her body around them. The eggs are very yolky, just like those of birds, and the babies inside feed on this nourishment until they hatch. The young then stay underground for up to four months where they are suckled by their mother.

To European explorers Australia seemed full of oddities and most of the animals were classed as rather primitive and inferior when compared with more conventional creatures in the rest of the world. The platypus, with its throwback to bird and reptile breeding, fitted this opinion very well. Strange they may be, but the modern view is that they are far from primitive. They have simply evolved solutions that are different to most other mammals. Take the males, for example. They are poisonous, one of only a handful of toxic mammals, but why?

The venom is held within a spur on the hind leg and for many years nobody had a clue what it was for. But the fact that only males have it, and that the venom glands increase in size in spring, suggests that it is associated with breeding. Males probably use it to deter competitors when seeking a mate or protecting their territory. Certainly males have been seen fighting during this period. They seem to try to wrap themselves around each other in a posture that would enable them to inject the venom into their opponent.

Adult platypus are about the size of a small cat and are voracious feeders, consuming up to a third of their body weight in a single night. They hunt caddis-fly and mayfly larvae, freshwater shrimps and other invertebrate life, and they can do this in fast-flowing rapids or stagnant pools as thick as pea soup. They can also find food in mud or under stones, and all this with their eyes and ears closed while underwater. So just how do they do it?

The key is their duck-like bill. It is soft, rubbery and covered in skin within which there are hundreds of tiny pits, arranged in rows. Scientific experiments have shown that these contain sensory organs. In fact, far more of the platypus's brain is devoted to the bill than to the eyes, ears, nose, tongue and rest of

the skin combined. It is a very important bit of kit, containing not only organs sensitive to touch but also a sixth sense: when an animal such as a shrimp moves its muscles, it emits tiny electrical fields that the platypus bill is able to detect. So the platypus can home in on a meal this way. Water flowing over a stream bed also sets up a pattern of electrical activity, so it is likely the platypus can navigate using this sense as well. If you watch one swimming, it moves its head from side to side, scanning as if with radar. In this way it is probably building up a complete three-dimensional picture of its world. This electrical sense is unique and has evolved independently of any other electrical senses in the animal kingdom. So the scientific view now is that the platypus is actually a very sophisticated animal, not primitive at all.

Relatively recent fossil discoveries have shown that platypus have also been in existence a very long time. A jaw bone 110 million years old shows that they were around at the time of the dinosaurs. That means they are older than the island of Australia itself! Today they are widespread right down the east coast – from Cooktown in the tropical north to Tasmania in the south – where the relatively wet climate provides many streams and rivers. They seem quite happy living in the steaming tropics or swimming under frozen lakes in the alps of Tasmania during winter. They are now even entering suburbia around the fringes of cities such as Melbourne. So in the future more Australians may be able to see and experience for themselves this unique Aussie icon.

1. Above water the platypus remains alert, with its eyes and ears open, but when submerged it closes both and relies on its electrical sense.

2. The platypus is completely at home underwater but in the wild rarely stays submerged for more than three minutes at a time.

DESERTS

Australia is the driest inhabited continent on Earth – almost half is desert, a larger proportion than any other continent. The vast dry centre has been called all kinds of names: the Outback, the Back of Beyond, the Never-Never, the Dead Heart. But while it was once maligned for its emptiness, intense heat and lack of water, it is now promoted as the very essence of Australia. Today, the endless dunes of the Simpson Desert and the shimmering white expanse of Lake Eyre are seen as places of unearthly beauty, and the world-famous Uluru has become the country's most exported image. This is a land of paradox: its mountains hide pockets of lush vegetation; the driest locations of all have oases of fish; and its rivers of sand can become raging torrents in just a few hours. The desert has become a symbol that now permeates the psyche of most Australians – the Red Centre, the Heart, the Soul of Australia.

Previous page: Dry rivers of sand, lined by river red gums, wind through Australia's centre.

DESERTS EVERYWHERE

Superficially, Australia's centre seems a sun-baked land of sandy deserts scattered with ancient crumbling mountain ranges. But it's very different to the well-known deserts of other countries, like Africa's Sahara or Namib with their enormous barren dunes, or the cactus-filled rocky deserts of the Americas. Sometimes it does not seem like a desert at all.

The desert ranges are cut by deep gorges that shelter pools of water where dingoes and a multitude of birds come to drink. Majestic river red gums line rivers of sand, their branches overloaded with noisy pink and grey galahs jostling for space. The rivers themselves snake through plains of woody shrubs, in places so dense they are difficult to walk through. Far from the ranges, sandy dunes roll to the horizon, their slopes dotted with sun-bleached grasses and colourful wildflowers.

This isn't the picture of a typical desert. Much of the centre is classified as desert simply because it has an average rainfall of less than 250 mm (10 inches) per year, but this average masks its erratic nature – months of flooding may alternate with years of drought. Australia's deserts experience the most highly variable and least predictable rainfall anywhere in the world. The arid zone of the Americas receives no more water, but it is predictable, so cacti and other succulents can survive the dry times by storing water in their leaves and stems and replenishing the supply every year. With no pattern of seasonal rains in Australia, succulents simply cannot survive.

As in other deserts, there are huge fluctuations in temperature, intensified by dry, cloudless skies. On summer days the temperature may soar to over 50°C (120°F), while winter nights can plummet to a freezing –8°C (18°F). The heat and dry air suck moisture out of everything. The soils are also extremely infertile, with nutrient levels about half those in other continents. Although this is tough on desert plants, they are surprisingly prolific, especially spinifex, a tall, spiky grass that covers a quarter of the centre. It is unlike any other grass: spiny, unpalatable, highly flammable and seeming to live almost on fresh air alone. The only large native grazer, the red kangaroo, cannot eat it.

Living in the desert

The desert's animals and plants must be able to withstand flood, drought, fire, heat and frost, and also draw nourishment from poor soils. To do this the unique array of wildlife has developed marvellous adaptations and strategies to enable it to endure bad times and then swiftly to grasp any opportunity, whenever and wherever it arises.

The bilby is a real symbol of the desert. It's a large bandicoot that lives in sandy areas, where it digs deep burrows. In many ways it is similar to a rabbit, with long ears and a loping gait, but the bilby has a long snout with sharp, pointed teeth and a long tail. At night it leaves its burrow to feed on insects and seeds. When there is abundant food it breeds prolifically, with up to three young in a litter, four times a year. Bilbies start breeding at just

six months. It's an efficient baby-production line and many desert animals have a similar breeding strategy, maximizing their numbers when conditions are good, replenishing small populations after deadly droughts.

The most important trick of desert survival is to reduce your need for water by sheltering from the heat. Many animals, like the bilby, are nocturnal and those that aren't seek shade during the hottest part of the day. Reptiles, insectivorous birds, many rodents and small carnivorous marsupials can live without drinking, extracting all the water they need from their food, and retaining fluid by concentrating their urine. Their problems are more about finding sufficient food and many of them are opportunistic feeders, eating whatever they can find.

Birds, being colourful and noisy, are

amongst the desert's most noticeable inhabitants and more than half are nomads, travelling to wherever there is rich plant growth, abundant insect activity or plentiful water. The centre is so varied that they can usually find a favourable area. Seed-eating budgerigars are amongst the most common desert nomads. They are rapid and acrobatic fliers and roam in small flocks, searching for seeding plants and water, which they need to drink every day.

Australia's deserts also contain an amazing variety of ants – they are everywhere. The exact number of species is not known, but it may be as high as 1000, as many as in some rainforests. They are so numerous that many plants have formed a partnership with them and rely on the ants for pollination and to disperse and germinate their seeds.

 BIG RED ROOS

Red kangaroos (left) bounding through the desert are the symbols of outback Australia. With males weighing up to 85 kg (190 pounds), they are Australia's largest native animal. Tolerant to heat, they are found throughout the centre except in the very driest deserts, usually in groups of a few females with joeys and a lingering red male. People used to think they were nomadic, but in reality they are territorial because it probably makes more sense to know where your food and water are instead of searching for them in the vast outback. Except in very hot weather, roos can go for several days without drinking, but they do need a supply of water or green vegetation, both of which greatly affect their population. During good years the female is a constant breeding machine with a joey at heel, a young in the pouch and a dormant embryo inside her. When the joey is weaned, the pouch young takes its place, and the embryo is born and enters the pouch. The female then mates and the cycle continues. During drought, males become sterile and the female's reproductive system shuts down. Many die in severe droughts, but when rains return the survivors can quickly resume breeding.

1. The flightless emu is Australia's largest bird, growing to over 1.5 m (5 feet) tall. If threatened they can sprint at speeds of up to 50 km (30 miles) an hour.

2. The bilby lives underground in deep burrows during the heat of the day. It has a marsupial pouch where its young spend their first two-and-a-half months.

⭐ The adult male red kangaroo can stand over 2 m (6 feet 6 inches) tall and reach 60 km (40 miles) an hour in bounds of 12 m (40 feet).

1. Termite mounds in the Tanami Desert. Termites are the miniature grazers of Australia; their total biomass is probably more than that of all the other animals living amongst spinifex.

2. The bizarre-looking thorny devil is a harmless, gentle lizard that only eats little black ants.

Overleaf: Spinifex or hummock grass dominates much of the centre.

The same but different

All of Australia's deserts are unified by a harsh climate, flatness and sand dunes, but each has a distinctive landscape. So although they merge one into the other with no definite boundaries, there are 10 different, recognizable deserts.

The Great Victoria Desert is the biggest, covering nearly 5 per cent of the continent. It merges with the Gibson and Great Sandy Deserts to form an enormous region of spinifex-coated sand dunes, salt lakes and shrublands, including the Nullarbor – a vast, treeless, limestone plateau the size of Great Britain, with large caves harbouring unique

cave life and underground lakes. Along the Great Australian Bight this plateau suddenly drops to the sea, forming spectacular sheer cliffs up to 120 m (390 feet) tall.

The Tanami Desert is a flat sand plain of spinifex frequently covered with thick scrub and trees such as hakeas and bloodwoods, a eucalypt named after its red sap. It has a higher rainfall than the other deserts and, where the soil is poorly drained, termites build their homes above ground. Their red mounds tower over the flat landscape and, with as many as 800 per hectare (over 300 per acre), the desert appears from a distance to be crowded with miniature skyscrapers.

Sturt Stony Desert is also distinctive. It is one of the most inhospitable places on the continent, with hot plains covered in a dense pavement of shimmering stones or gibbers. These are rounded by wind-blown sand, and a desert varnish of iron oxide and silica gives them a polished, red-brown appearance. Yet several animals specialize in this habitat, such as the gibberbird, which lives amongst the stones all year round, even when the rocks reach a baking 70°C (160°F).

Perhaps the classic desert is the Simpson, the most arid of all, but with a wide variety of landscapes that support large populations of mammals, birds and lizards.

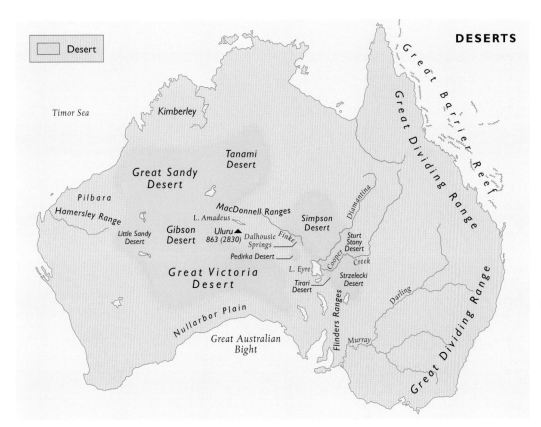

DESERTS

2

 THE MARSUPIAL MOLE

One of the enigmas of the Australian desert, this small, silky-furred mammal (left), about 14 cm (less than 6 inches) long, survives by spending its whole life in sand. Only occasionally after rain has it been seen on the surface, drinking or eating a few termites, before rapidly disappearing back into the sand. It is also impossible to keep in captivity. This means the marsupial mole is one of the least understood mammals in the world. We don't even know how males and females find each other, as they appear to live solitary lives. They're well suited to their burrowing lifestyle, with a horny shield protecting the nose, and fused vertebrae in the neck allowing the head to be used as a ramrod. The huge front paws have spade-like claws, useful for rapid digging. They have no eyes or external ears, but have a good sense of smell. A backward-opening pouch is present in both sexes, although better developed in females. This mole doesn't have permanent tunnels – it virtually swims through the sand, which collapses behind it so that no tunnel remains. Day or night, it hunts through the sand for insect eggs and larvae, feeding voraciously, then suddenly dropping into a deep sleep, before becoming frantically active again.

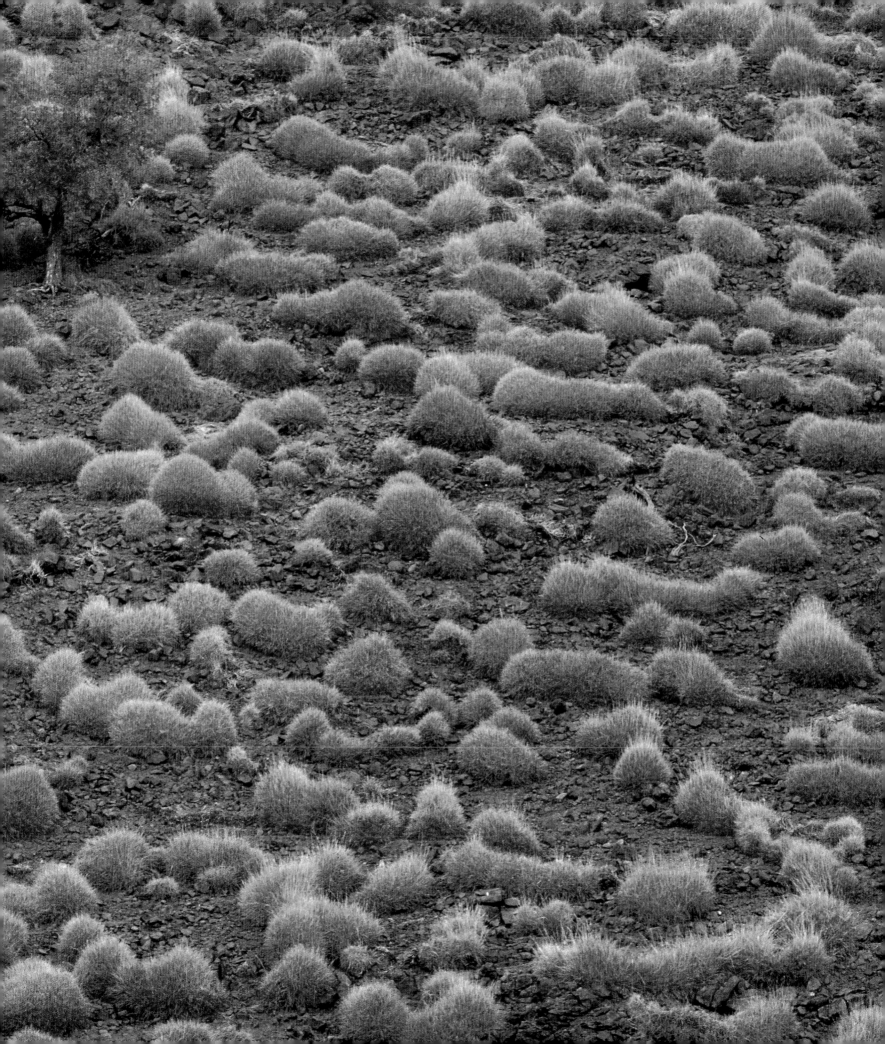

1

THE SIMPSON DESERT

Located within the driest region of the continent, the Simpson is immense. It is the largest sand-ridge desert in the world, covering an area of 176,500 sq. km (68,200 square miles), over five times the size of Belgium, an endless vista of more than 1100 parallel sand dunes running for hundreds of kilometres, all oriented in a northwesterly direction. Some are up to 40 m (130 feet) high and over 200 km (125 miles) long. The south also harbours a complex of dry salt lakes, ephemeral gems that fill during rare floods. The Simpson literally soaks up rivers, which disappear into its sands, none ever reaching its arid heart. Most

years it receives less than 100 mm (4 inches) of rain and it's possible that parts of it experience the hottest temperatures in Australia, over 50°C (120°F), but there is no one in the desert to measure them.

Aboriginal people lived here for thousands of years, but the first white explorers called it the Dead Heart and avoided it. So its nature remained unknown to Europeans until 1936, when it was finally crossed by a local pastoralist with an Aboriginal companion. Today, the Simpson remains one of the most remote and empty landscapes in the centre.

However, far from being a barren land of wind-swept sand, the Simpson is a richly vegetated, living desert. Sandhill canegrass is

one of the few plants to grow on the ever-moving dune crests that are constantly blown and sculpted by the wind. It stabilizes the sand and provides homes for small desert animals such as the Eyrean grasswren that scampers between the wiry clumps, crushing canegrass seeds with its finch-like bill. Spinifex grows on more stable slopes and between the dunes, where it is essential for the survival of desert skinks. Slender and secretive lizards, they can easily wriggle through spinifex, and quickly disappear into its prickly clumps when disturbed. Hunters find the spiky shield difficult to penetrate, so the skinks have a safe haven.

Scattered between the dunes are drought-

2

tolerant woodlands of mulga, desert oak and gidgee that provide nest sites and strategic perches for wedge-tailed eagles and other birds of prey. Their acute eyes are sensitive to movement and once they spot their prey they lock on to it and attack in a swift glide from their perch. Reptiles make up the bulk of their food, but now introduced rabbits have become an important item on their menu, especially after good rains when the desert swarms with them.

Desert rains also create plagues of native rats and these are the favourite prey of letter-winged kites, beautiful white birds of prey with black-trimmed wings. They hunt at night and when the numbers of rats soar, the kites gather in their hundreds and breed, relying on the plagues to boost their population.

After rain, colourful wildflowers carpet the dunes with splashes of white, yellow, pink, purple and blue. Extensive clusters of poached-egg daisies are some of the most spectacular, their large white and yellow heads reaching up over 50 cm (20 inches). Beautiful butterflies, beetles and native wasps are attracted to the pollen and nectar, and small caterpillars and bugs quickly start to devour the blooms. The flowers blossom only briefly, but they renew the vitality of the desert, producing masses of seeds that will lie dormant in the sand until the next unpredictable rainstorm.

1. The sand dunes of the Simpson started to form around 18,000 years ago when incessant winds piled sand into long dunes.

2. The wedge-tailed eagle is Australia's largest bird of prey, and is commonly seen fighting over carcasses alongside the centre's roads.

ANCIENT OUTBACK

Compared with the rest of the world, relatively few major geological events have disturbed the surface of Australia, so the continent retains a fabulous record of our planet's history. One of the reasons is that the land of Australia sits right at the centre of its own continental plate, with a buffer of surrounding islands to the north and east, so the mainland itself is not colliding and crunching with any other part of the Earth. The continental crust is also relatively thick, so the hot molten rock beneath the surface can rarely break through and cause volcanic eruptions. With such a calm continental surface it's perhaps not surprising that almost anywhere you look in outback Australia you can find evidence of ancient rocks and landscapes, preserved until the present.

2

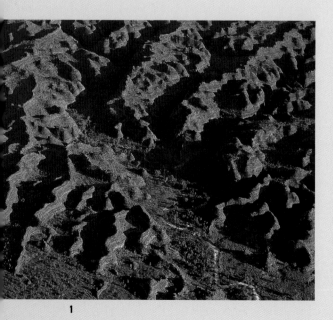

1

One of the most magical rock formations of all is the Bungle Bungle Range in Purnululu National Park in the Kimberley region of the far northwest. They stand as thousands upon thousands of grey- and orange-striped beehive domes towering 250 m (820 feet) above the surrounding plain. The sandstone from which they are formed was deposited about 360 million years ago, but the towers themselves have been shaped by streams and rivers in just the last 20 million years. The strange dark bands, which are created by primitive bacteria, have appeared since then so, although these mystical structures appear timeless, they are relative youngsters by Australian standards.

Even Uluru, or Ayers Rock, the most famous icon of Australia, is not amongst the continent's oldest formations. It was originally laid down as sand in an ancient sea over 500 million years ago and then tilted up into its present position about 300 million years later to become the world's largest single rock – 348 m (1141 feet) high and more than 9 km (6 miles) around its base. In fact this is just the tip of a vast 'underground mountain' that extends a further 6 km (4 miles) beneath the desert.

To start travelling seriously back in time there are few better locations than the rugged escarpments of Kakadu National Park in the Top End. Here you can walk on rocks

rocks that date back 3.7 billion years, making them the oldest in Australia, and elsewhere in Western Australia lie some of the earliest remains of life on Earth. At a blisteringly hot location – curiously called North Pole because it is so remote – there are fossils of bacterial pillars called stromatolites that date back 3.5 billion years. Nearby, at Narryer, crystals of the mineral zircon have been discovered that are 4.2 billion years old. The Earth itself formed only about 4.5 billion years ago, so Australia has geology that reaches back almost to the beginning of our planet's existence.

1. The sandstone of the Bungle Bungle Ranges in Purnululu National Park has been eroded into a spectacular maze of ridges and beehive domes.

2. The unusual banding on the Bungle Bungle domes is caused by alternating coatings of cyanobacteria and iron oxide.

3. Joffre Gorge in Karijini National Park has been carved out from rock that is a staggering 2.5 billion years old.

that were originally laid down as sandstone and conglomerate in rivers and shallow seas over 1.5 billion years ago. These lie over even older metamorphic rocks which contain rich deposits of uranium. For most of the last 1.5 billion years this region has been remarkably stable, so water has been able to sculpt the landscape into the fabulous cliffs, crags and river valleys you see today.

For large areas of really ancient geology the best place by far is Western Australia: there are few more awesome locations on Earth than the dramatic gorges of Karijini National Park in the Pilbara region. They plunge vertically into the desert plains, at times their walls no more than an arm's width apart. Descending into their narrow, twisting depths is to travel 2.5 billion years into the past, when their bright red rocks were originally formed. This was a time when the Earth's primitive algae were first producing oxygen. The red colour in the rocks is rust, created when iron-rich sediments were contaminated by an atmosphere newly full of oxygen. The numerous gorges snake through the desert, creating a fascinating maze in which it is easy to lose sense of space and time, and every year people lose their way in this mesmerizing world of rock and water.

In other parts of the Pilbara there are

⬥ TOPIC LINKS

2.2 Red Centre
p. 68 Uluru and Kata Tjuta

3.3 The Top End
p. 110 Kakadu

4.1 Tropical Seas
p. 130 Shark Bay

DESERT NIGHTS

In the middle of the day the dunes seem barren of life. The burning sun forces many birds and even sun-loving reptiles into shade, and nearly three-quarters of all the mammals will be underground, avoiding heat stress in their burrows. Even big red kangaroos can be almost invisible, lying under bushes and moving only occasionally to dig for cooler ground or to lick their forearms for some relief from the heat.

However, take a walk in the evening with a torch and you'll see the dunes come alive as the night shift emerges. You'll notice tiny green lights glinting in the sand – the eyes of wolf spiders reflecting the torchlight, betraying their position. They are hunting for insects. Scorpions also hunt at this time, but often prefer to wait patiently at their burrow entrance until their prey blunders by.

Subtle sounds fill the air: the whirr of crickets; stridulating spiders; the high-pitched squeaks of bats echolocating insect prey, and the 'geck-ko' of geckos, the only lizards with a voice. Because of their soft skin they come out only in the coolness of the night. They are enchanting creatures, with large, smiling mouths and huge, lidless eyes that they clean and moisten with the swipe of a fat tongue.

Most animals appear only after sunset because this helps reduce their need for precious water. Small marsupial carnivores, like dunnarts and mulgaras, can survive without drinking, as their prey provides them with sufficient fluids, but seed-eaters such as the spinifex hopping-mouse have a tougher time. This long-legged burrower is one of the most common rodents in the desert, and possibly the most arid-adapted animal in the world. Remarkably, it gets all the water it needs from the breakdown of carbohydrates in dry seeds and it also has incredibly efficient kidneys that conserve water by creating the most concentrated urine ever recorded for a mammal.

It can be difficult to tell the difference between these small rodents and some of the carnivorous marsupials for which Australia's deserts are famous. Despite their size, their battles for survival are no less ferocious than those of the big cats of Africa. The smallest, the wongai ningaui, is no bigger than a man's thumb, but it fearlessly tackles almost anything, even lizards larger than itself, biting them furiously around the head till they succumb. The largest of these small hunters is the mulgara, which is 10 times larger than a wongai ningaui. In fact it sometimes eats other marsupials, although beetles and lizards are more common prey. Like all the little carnivorous marsupials it stores fat in its broad tail as a buffer against food shortage – a good strategy in the unpredictable desert.

It's amazing how active these tiny marsupials are. Dunnarts have hairy feet which act rather like snowshoes, preventing them from sinking into the sand and allowing them to move swiftly over the dunes. On a typical evening a dunnart will leave its burrow and scurry to a dune crest to hunt, listening and sniffing for insects, spiders and small reptiles. It captures them with its front paws and then devours them with almost manic urgency. There is little cover up here and, although prey is easier to see, the dunnart is also exposed. Often it will dare to stay several hours, always on the move, before returning to the cover of vegetation at the base of the dune to rest. Before dawn it will make the journey again for another hunt and in the course of a night this tiny creature, weighing just 15 g ($^1/_2$ ounce), may travel as much as 3 km ($1^1/_2$ miles).

In the morning the dunes will be quiet again, but covered in numerous tracks and a few half-eaten insects, the only evidence of a busy night.

1. The mulgara does not need to drink but obtains moisture from the food it eats.

2. The spinifex hopping-mouse population can erupt into thousands when there is a super-abundance of food.

3. Australian scorpions can reach a length of 12 cm (5 inches) but none has venom that is fatal to humans.

1

The desert atmosphere is so clean and dry that on a clear desert night, with a full moon, the light is bright enough to read by.

3

REALM OF THE REPTILE

Reptiles are superbly adapted to the desert's unpredictable conditions. With a low metabolic rate they don't need to eat as often as warm-blooded animals and when food is scarce or temperatures too hot or too cold, they become inactive, virtually switching off to save energy. Reptiles do not have to drink; they can obtain all their moisture needs from their food, though many will drink if water is available. They're so successful here that the reptile fauna is more diverse than in any other habitat on Earth and Australia's deserts are particularly famous for their abundance of lizards.

In spinifex grasslands there can be over 400 lizards in every hectare (160 in every acre), from over 40 different species – more species than in the whole of Europe. Lizards, and their success, are directly related to spinifex and the hoards of termites that eat it. In places like the Tanami, termite mounds are the equivalent of enormous herds of stationary herbivores as far as the predatory lizards are concerned. The termites are at least part of the diet of most of the lizards – the dragons, nocturnal geckos, legless lizards, smaller goannas and especially the skinks. Many, like the sand-swimming skinks, break into sub-terranean termite tunnels. They live underground and have no need of legs, so their limbs are reduced to mere stumps or flaps. The beaked gecko is also a termite specialist. When hunting, it tilts its head from side to side listening for them, then wriggles into the sand to break open the tunnels.

While lizards often eat large amounts of termites, they are opportunistic feeders. Some, such as the centralian blue-tongue, also eat bits of vegetation and flowers. Others take whatever prey they can find, like the ornate skink that just sticks its head out of its burrow and grabs whatever comes by. Thorny devils, on the other hand, are real specialists and can usually be found near trails of tiny black ants, their only source of food. Some lizards even eat each other. Burton's legless lizard, common in the Simpson, feeds almost entirely on skinks. It hides in leaf litter, wriggling its tail to attract prey, or drapes itself on spinifex on which it sometimes impales its victim. Knob-tailed geckos feast on smaller geckos, but they too can become victims and if threatened they raise their bodies high off the ground, arch their backs like angry cats and leap forward, uttering wheezing, dog-like barks. It's all bluff, but it often works.

The centre's top predators are the voracious monitors with their ripping claws, sharp teeth and long spiny tails which they use as whips to knock attackers off their feet. The giant perentie grows up to 2.5 m (8 feet) long and is the world's second largest lizard, after the Komodo dragon of Indonesia. It often lives in rocky outcrops where it uses keen

1

2

1. The biggest lizard in Australia is the perentie. Large adults are virtually fearless with blade-like claws and sharp teeth.

2. Often mistaken for a snake, Burton's legless lizard belongs to a family of lizards found only in Australasia. It feeds on other lizards, especially skinks.

3. The smooth knob-tailed gecko has no eyelids and a fat tail which ends in a small knob.

eyesight and smell to survey the surrounding country for prey. The smaller but more common sand goanna eats virtually anything it can catch and swallow, including carrion. Spencer's monitor likes living dangerously and preys on smaller snakes such as death adders. This goanna cleverly avoids the first strike, then grabs the serpent while it is off balance and before it has a chance to strike again.

Snakes also occur throughout the deserts. Some are harmless, like the four types of python, but compared with the rest of the world a greater number of Australia's species are elapids, front-fanged and venomous, with some of the deadliest venoms in the world. Nearly 70 per cent of the desert snakes belong to this family. The particularly potent venom

may be a way of ensuring that every strike will be successful in an environment where prey animals can be few and far between. For people in the desert there is some comfort in knowing that snake encounters are rare, as most snakes shy away from humans.

Australia's inland taipan is the deadliest snake in the world and although it is some-times called the fierce snake that name contradicts its shy and secretive habits. It often hunts in a labyrinth of dry, cracked clay where native long-haired rats and tiny planigales shelter from the hot sun. The deadly venom ensures the taipan will catch a meal every time because each bite, provided venom is injected, is sure to be fatal. Even if the victim is able to run before it dies, it won't get far and the snake can follow its trail and locate it with ease.

◆ TOPIC LINKS

2.1 Red Centre
p. 58 Desert nights

5.2 Pacific Jewels
p. 176 New Caledonia –
a glimpse into the past

5.3 New Zealand
p. 189 Island refuges

6.2 Living with Wildlife
p. 208 Dangerous Australians

RED CENTRE

Almost everywhere in the centre red is a predominant theme and the clear skies and powerful sun intensify the radiant ochres, oranges, purples and other variants of this colour. Whilst the red dunes of the Simpson and the red dome of Uluru are the desert's icons, the mountains are even more vivid. They include the Hamersley Range near the west coast and the MacDonnell, James and Musgrave Ranges in the centre.

As in the ancient regions of Western Australia, the red is caused by iron in the rocks turning to rust when it comes into contact with oxygen. As the mountains wear away, sand is produced, which also turns red and so gives the entire centre its characteristic colour. Breakaways – flat-topped, low-lying hills – add extra hues. These white and ochre hills crumble into extensive plains of rust-coated rocks and their brilliant colours at sunrise and sunset make this one of the most striking landscapes in the centre.

DESERT MOUNTAINS

The most dramatic feature of Australia's desert heart is the rugged mountain range rising from an otherwise flat land. The MacDonnell Ranges are the second highest mountains on the continent, exceeded only by the Great Dividing Range. Even so, their highest peak, Mount Zeil, is only 1531 m (5022 feet). When they were first pushed up, over 310 million years ago, their ridges rose more than 9 km (6 miles) into the sky, but these are now some of the oldest mountains in the world and have been weather-beaten to a crumbling skeleton. The debris from this erosion has created the extensive plains and sand dunes to the south, including the vast Simpson Desert.

What they lack in height, the MacDonnells easily make up for in spectacularly beautiful scenery and varied life. Their 400-km (250-mile) length is carved with numerous gorges, ancient cuttings made by creeks and rivers. Many of the deep canyons hold moisture all year round and allow water-loving plants to flourish. Palm Valley is named after a stand of unique cabbage palms, remnants of the luxuriant rainforest that covered Australia some 65 million years ago. Today, these slender palms are found nowhere else in the world and their closest relatives are over 1000 km (625 miles) away. Thousands of them grow from the

1. A series of rugged parallel ridges, the MacDonnell Ranges are one of the oldest ranges in the world.

1

valley floor, their green tops rustling in the breeze 30 m (100 feet) above. Giant fern-like cycads that evolved during the time of the dinosaurs grow on the shady valley walls and reed-fringed pools ripple with insects, between stands of palms. This lush oasis exists because the mountain rocks store water like a sponge. It gradually seeps out long after the brief and unpredictable rains have ended, forming pools of precious water.

Crevices and caves within the precipitous gorges shelter small groups of black-footed rock wallabies. They are remarkably agile, bounding up and down sheer cliff faces at astonishing speed. This keeps them one jump ahead of predatory dingoes and wedge-tailed eagles. But there is not much food on the rocky walls, so in the cooler mornings and evenings the wallabies

venture out onto the grassy slopes to eat or drink.

Although there are few permanent pools, the dry riverbeds contain underground water and large trees can tap into this, so the riverbanks are lined with shady tea-trees, coolibahs and towering river red gums. These, in turn, provide homes for a multitude of birds, particularly noisy parrots, cockatoos and ubiquitous black crows. The centre of Australia may be a desert, but it supports more species of birds than the whole of Britain. Surprisingly, more than half of them do not need to drink, but the waterholes in the ranges are especially important for those that do. These are mostly the seed-eating birds such as zebra finches, pigeons and parrots that cannot obtain enough moisture in their diet. Most birds drink in the early

morning or late afternoon but, to avoid congestion, different species fly in at slightly different times so there is a continual procession of life to the water's edge.

The MacDonnells are also important for wildlife far away from their rocky peaks. Much of the centre receives less than 200 mm (8 inches) of rain a year, usually in brief, irregular falls. The mountains funnel rainwater, concentrating it into creeks and rivers that flow out of the ranges, thus sending water and nutrients into the desert. During drought many plants and animals can survive only in these mountain fortresses and disperse to recolonize the desert when conditions improve. So the mountains are a refuge for life, their sheltered gorges and waterholes creating important oases in an otherwise arid land.

⭐ Red dust from the desert can travel enormous distances to land on the mountains of New Zealand or to the Southern Ocean, where it fertilizes the sea.

1

1. A female dingo has only one litter a year. An average of five pups are born during winter in large dens that are often close to water.

2. (opposite) The red cabbage palms in Palm Valley are living fossils from the time when tropical forests covered most of the continent.

Overleaf: The famous western face of Kata Tjuta glows in the afternoon sun. These domes are sacred to Aboriginal people.

ULURU AND KATA TJUTA

The continent's centre holds two of the world's most famous rock formations – Uluru and Kata Tjuta, once called Ayers Rock and the Olgas. For Australians, as well as many international visitors, travelling to Uluru is almost like a pilgrimage and each evening huge numbers of people watch the rock change colour at sunset. To the traditional owners, the Anangu people, Uluru and Kata Tjuta are full of spiritual meaning and central to their lives. The rock formations provide evidence of the creation of life, including their ancestors, and this forms the basis for the Tjukurpa – the collection of history, knowledge, religion and morality that guides the Anangu's daily lives.

The gigantic rounded monolith of Uluru, 'the great pebble', rises sheer from a sandy plain, dwarfing everything nearby, and is all the more imposing because it stands alone. In the distant west rise the mysterious domes of Kata Tjuta, whose name means 'many heads' in the Anangu language. A collection of giant red domes carved with gorges and valleys, Kata Tjuta covers a larger area than Uluru and its tallest dome, Mount Olga, rises to 546 m (1791 feet), so many people consider it even more impressive.

The best way to experience the sheer size and bulk of Uluru is to take a walk around its base, amongst the tall bloodwoods and acacias that fringe it. It has a weather-beaten face sculpted with caves of all sizes, large honeycombed hollows and smaller pits. Waterworn ridges resembling ribs create long vertical shadows and cascading potholes form dry waterfalls of rock. Gorges hide waterholes shaded by trees and shrubs where wildflowers grow, birds and dingoes come to drink and lizards bask in the sun. All around its base are fallen boulders, some larger than a house. Close up, the surface is

1

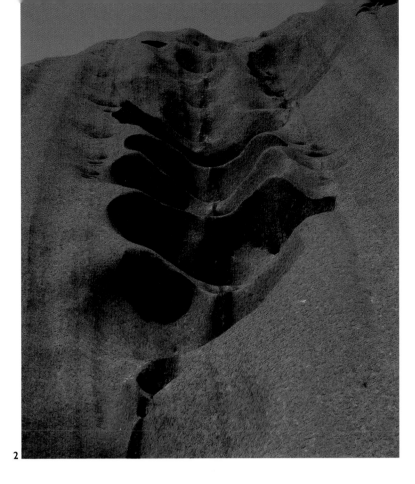

2

1. More of Uluru is being revealed as the sand blows away from the surrounding desert. About two-thirds of it is still underground.

2. The constant erosion of Uluru has created a dramatic surface.

Grains of sand are produced by cycles of mountain building and erosion. They are resistant to breakdown and therefore most of central Australia is covered in sand.

rough, covered in angular overlapping flakes shaped by the action of wind, rain and chemical decay. Occasionally a flake of rusty sandstone falls off to reveal its underlying hue of muddy grey.

Kata Tjuta's broad domes glow with the sun's first light, but the valleys remain dark until later in the day, when the sun is higher. The domes all lean slightly towards each other and on the top of some of them enough soil and water is trapped for grasses and wattles to grow. From a distance the slopes appear smooth, but they are actually made up of a conglomerate of rocks and boulders of many sizes.

Rain extinguishes the red glow of both Uluru and Kata Tjuta, darkening them to sombre browns, but at this time they also come alive, as grooves and channels fill with water that pours off in a series of waterfalls. The sound of the roaring water is deafening. When it rains you are witnessing the power of water that, over millions of years, has sculpted these rocks into their dramatic modern shapes.

The red domes of Uluru and Kata Tjuta are the visible tips of slabs of sedimentary rock that extend up to 6 km (4 miles) beneath the ground. The original sediments were washed into a huge inland sea over 500 million years ago and the same mountain-building forces that squeezed up the MacDonnell Ranges also thrust these rocks up, so the horizontal layers of Uluru were tilted almost vertical. This can be seen today because the layers have eroded unevenly, leaving distinctive vertical ridges and furrows. Kata Tjuta's conglomerate was only slightly tilted, but suffered a number of gigantic fractures; subsequent weathering widened these fissures into canyons and valleys, eroding the mass into the familiar multitude of domes.

The surrounding desert is sandy but there's not a bare dune in sight except during droughts. It's covered in thick vegetation. Sun-bleached grasses cover most of the dunes and honey grevilleas are one of the most conspicuous plants. Their flowers grow on long spikes and are sweet with nectar that you can easily

suck into your mouth. Over 170 different types of birds live in the area, with many, such as painted firetails and spotted bowerbirds, preferring the wide wooded valleys of Kata Tjuta where they can find food, water and shelter. Spotted bowerbird males build elaborate bowers of finely interwoven twigs and grass which they decorate with bleached bones, stones, berries and even glass in order to attract a mate. They are also accomplished mimics, copying the calls of other birds, and when a female appears they launch into an animated display, dancing and singing to encourage her to mate. The sand plains are also home to the great desert skink, which lives in large family burrows. The skinks leave piles of scats at the burrow entrance to stake out their territory and will fight with any other lizards that try to move into their spacious dwellings. They will even attack mammals if they try to take over their burrows.

With its living desert and mystical monoliths this area is truly one of the most remarkable places on Earth.

Desert rain is rare, unpredictable and often localized, and when it does fall much of the water evaporates in the heat or soaks rapidly into the sand. After disappearing underground this moisture is stored in the soil, particularly in streambeds and floodplains where plant roots can tap into it long after water has vanished from the surface. The movement of this underground water connects the different desert regions, bringing life to places far from the original rain. When the rivers flow, waterholes are revived and floodwaters are carried great distances to create ephemeral wetlands full of life. Heavy rains recharge the water table and springs occur where ground water meets the surface, creating oases in the desert with an amazing diversity of life. Rains also trigger spectacular, if relatively brief, spurts of plant growth, which in turn support far more wildlife than you would expect in a place where water is so scarce.

THE FINKE RIVER

The Finke is the biggest river in the centre – 690 km (430 miles) from its headwaters in the west MacDonnell Ranges to its floodout in the Simpson Desert. Like many rivers in Australia, it does not empty into the sea but meanders inland towards the sump of the centre, Lake Eyre. This river owes its existence to the central ranges that funnel meagre rains into creeks which flow into the Finke maybe only once a year. The Finke rarely flows over its entire length and after rain its modest stream subsides within a few days to leave a ribbon of sand punctuated by the occasional waterhole. Surprisingly, much of it has followed the same course for almost 350 million years, making it the oldest river in the world.

Because rain is rare the Finke is important in redistributing water and nutrients through the desert. Even when dry, it stores water deep in its sand and this nurtures a band of gum trees, over a kilometre (2/3 mile) wide in parts, creating a vibrant river of green across the arid centre. These gum trees are full of life: fairy martins build intricate mud nests on their trunks, while white-plumed honey-eaters glean sugary secretions from their flowers and colourful ring-necked parrots, galahs and red-tailed black cockatoos roost in the branches and nest in their hollows.

To the Aboriginal people, this is Larapinta, meaning 'salty water', a river rich in history. Its permanent waterholes and wide flat bed not only provided water and food, it was a travel route through the desert. The first European explorers also used the Finke as a navigation aid and white settlers established pastoral settlements around its reliable pools.

The permanent waterholes are home to fish, freshwater crayfish and shrimps. Mussels live in the sediments and move by anchoring their large fleshy foot into the mud and hauling themselves along. The desert's aquatic creatures survive the dry times here and then explode into life when rains come, multiplying and dispersing with the flood-waters to repopulate the river and lakes.

1. Noisy galahs are often found around the Finke's waterholes.

⭐ None of the rivers in central Australia ever reaches the ocean.

1. The normally dry Finke River quickly becomes a raging torrent following heavy rains.

2. (opposite) Budgerigars are desert nomads that fly long distances in search of food and water.

The Finke is responsible for a dramatic landscape. Palm Valley with its famous cabbage palms and cycads runs into the Finke Gorge, a 65-km (40-mile) long area of steep valleys, sheer cliffs and dramatic amphitheatres sculpted by the river's prehistoric meanderings.

Just downstream, Boggy Hole is a paradox in the desert – a large, spring-fed waterhole shaded by lofty red gums and sandstone bluffs. More than 200 types of birds have been seen here, particularly migratory waterbirds. It seems strange to see ducks, grebes, cormorants and large pelicans in the centre of the desert. Nomadic black swans are occasionally even spotted resting at the waterhole

before continuing their journey.

Out of the ranges, the Finke snakes through mulga woodlands and some of the richest grazing land in central Australia. Roughly halfway from its headwaters, the river is a kilometre (2/3 mile) wide band of sand that forms the western edge of the Simpson Desert. Giant sand dunes rise along its banks. The surrounding country is also covered in flat-topped breakaways, the remains of an ancient plateau.

Further south, the infrequent flows that reach this far spread into the Finke floodout – an enormous web of channels and swamps amongst impenetrable woodlands of eucalypts and shrubs. This is an important

refuge for life, particularly during drought, but eventually the trees thin out and the Finke finally disappears into the sand dunes of the Simpson.

Every decade or so, when rains are particularly heavy, the Finke will flow its entire length. The raging waters sweep aside giant trees and boulders, heaping debris high into the treetops. The water may spread far beyond the river's poorly marked banks to flood more than 10,000 sq. km (3900 square miles) of desert, as happened in 1974, 1988 and 2000. Some people say that during really big floods the Finke flows right through the Simpson's dunes and beyond, eventually reaching its prehistoric outlet at Lake Eyre.

THE GREAT ARTESIAN BASIN

In the middle of thousands of square kilometres of desert you find large pools of warm water, fringed with reeds, bulrushes, tea-trees and date palms. On a cold winter morning thick steam rises in plumes and glows in the sun's early rays. Coots glide out of the mist and tiny variegated fairy wrens perch in bushes near the water's edge, warming up in the steam. With no wind, the mist envelops the pool and its plants, hiding them in thick fog. These are the famous Dalhousie mound springs.

The water here originally fell as rain 1500 km (1000 miles) away nearly 2 million years ago, and comes from a huge underground store called the Great Artesian Basin. This is one of the largest groundwater basins in the world, underlying 1.76 million sq. km (687,500 square miles) – that's almost a quarter of Australia – and estimated to store about 4400 million Olympic-sized swimming pools of water. It is ironic that this unimaginable volume of water lies beneath the desert. The water is held at depths reaching 1500 m (almost a mile), in layers of porous sandstone that act like a sponge, sandwiched between layers of impervious rock. Along the eastern margins of the basin, near the Great Dividing Range, the sandstone comes to the surface, allowing rainwater to percolate in. This water moves slowly downhill through the porous rock at an average of between 1 and 5 m (3 and 16 feet) a year and so it takes over a million years to reach the lowest part of Australia, Lake Eyre.

Along the western side of the basin the water pushes up through faults in the rock creating springs that bubble and gush out onto the surface. The greatest concentration of springs is found at Dalhousie, on the western edge of the Simpson Desert, where a 70-sq. km (27-square mile) area of large pools and creeks is maintained by an enormous natural discharge of artesian water emerging at temperatures of 30–46°C (86–115°F). Six kinds of fish live here and one, called the Dalhousie hardyhead, survives in water hotter than almost any other fish in the world is able to bear. It darts in and out of hot water bubbling up from the bottom of pools to feed on stirred up algae, detritus and small inverte-

1. Red kangaroos are more abundant since the discovery of the Great Artesian Basin.

2. A large pool of warm water at Dalhousie Springs is fed from a natural discharge of the Great Artesian Basin.

brates. The pools are extraordinary, isolated oases with fish, plants and other wildlife found nowhere else on Earth, and many desert animals also visit the springs to quench their thirst.

It is not just wildlife that lives on artesian water; people have also tapped into it. Following its discovery in 1878, many boreholes were drilled and the arid centre was opened up to human habitation and grazing stock. Wildlife has also benefited: red kangaroos are more abundant today than before European settlement and water-loving corellas can always be found around outback homesteads. Unfortunately, the water is being used up faster than it can be replenished, endangering the delicate balance of this wonderful resource.

2

▷ CAMELS

Australia is the only country where you'll find wild populations of one-humped camels (left). All the camels in the Middle East and Africa are domesticated to some extent. European endeavour in Australia owes much to the camel. Some 12,000 of them, imported between 1840 and 1907, provided reliable transport to people pioneering the interior. Some escaped and many were released in the mid-1920s when they were superseded by motor vehicles. They established free-ranging herds throughout the centre and now number over 500,000 – a huge population that almost makes them a serious pest. They are brilliantly adapted for desert life and, with no natural enemies or serious diseases, have few factors limiting their population growth in Australia's deserts. Camels are browsers and can eat over 80 per cent of the centre's plant species. Highly mobile, they move an average of 3 km (2 miles) per day, searching for the freshest vegetation. When the moisture content of plants is high they can exist for several months without drinking, and can even drink salt water. However, camels do perish during droughts when there is little food and no surface water.

1

SALT LAKES

A striking feature of central Australia is the number of clay pans and salt lakes, some just a few metres across, others several kilometres wide. Most salt lakes appear dry with a crusty surface of salt, but deep mud often lies below the surface. Millions of years ago the sea often invaded huge areas of the interior, leaving salt behind, which later accumulated in low-lying areas, creating salt lakes. Salt is also blown in from the sea, carried by air masses as they move inland and then deposited with rain.

Lake Eyre is Australia's largest salt lake, situated in the driest region of the country. More than any other feature in the desert, it helped give the arid zone its barren reputation. Early European explorers thought a landmass as large as Australia must have an inland sea. In 1840 Edward John Eyre became the first European to see the salt lakes and stared in horror at 'one vast, low and dreary waste'. Successive explorers were even more disapproving: Major P. Egerton Warburton remarked, 'Lake Eyre was terrible in its death-like stillness and the vast expanse of its unbroken sterility.'

2

Lake Eyre is a 9000-sq. km (3000-square mile) pan of salt and clay. It is the lowest point on the continent, at 15 m (50 feet) below sea level, and is actually made up of two lakes connected by a narrow channel. A northern part, near the mouth of the main inlet, is covered with clay and only a powder of salt. The rest has a salt crust, possibly the largest area of salt coating in the world, covering over 2500 sq. km (1000 square miles). In some areas it is 50 cm (20 inches) thick and, although solid enough to support a locomotive, floats on a great sea of mud up to 6 m (20 feet) thick.

It would appear as though nothing lives on the lake, but the Lake Eyre dragon is found nowhere else. This little lizard, about 7 cm (3 inches) long, spends almost its entire life amongst the salt crust, feeding mainly on black harvester ants. It often walks on its heels to protect its toes from the heat and shelters beneath the cracking salt. It can exist in one of the harshest environments on Earth by burrowing down into the moist mud during very hot conditions, and when the lake fills it simply moves ashore.

Lake Eyre is part of the largest internal drainage system in the world, draining one-sixth of Australia. Major river systems carry water in from areas of higher and more reliable rainfall and occasionally discharge enough water to fill the lake and dissolve the salt. When it fills the water spreads out to become Australia's largest lake. It has been completely flooded only three times in the last century, but the lake fills partially every five to 10 years. Much has been written about the spectacle of flood when the 'dead heart' comes to life. An ethereal sight, it's difficult to tell where the water stops and the sky begins. There is something about very saline water that enhances reflections; a mirror-smooth surface reflects clouds and sunlight in the most amazing fashion.

The inflowing water is full of life – bacteria and algae, crustaceans, molluscs and insects. Millions of fish flood in from rivers and breed – up to 25 different species, including bony bream, yellowbelly, hardyheads and catfish. Then, as the water evaporates and salinity increases, the different fish species die out one at a time according to their salt tolerance, and form thick bands of dead bodies around the shore. The Lake Eyre hardyheads are the last fish to die. But the toughest animals are the primitive crustaceans – the shield and brine shrimps that can tolerate conditions 10 times saltier than sea water. Their drought-resistant eggs remain buried in the salt crust and hatch when the lake is next flooded.

All this life feeds an amazing number of birds. Within days of water entering the lake hundreds and even thousands of water birds fly in from all over the country – Australian pelicans, banded stilts, terns and silver gulls. No-one knows how the birds become aware that the lake is filling; perhaps they sense changes in atmospheric pressure or can smell water. They rapidly start breeding on low-lying islands. The banded stilts and pelicans form huge colonies of tens of thousands and keep on breeding until their food disappears. The fish-eating pelicans feed on the lake and also on the surrounding flooded rivers, then fly back to their chicks to disgorge their meals. Large crèches of floating stilt chicks feed on brine shrimp in the company of protective males, while the females incubate more eggs.

The early explorers were correct – there is an inland sea, just not quite as they had imagined it, and it has taken over 200 years for non-indigenous Australians really to appreciate this amazing natural wonder.

1. Lake Amadeus is a 500-km (300-mile) long chain of salt lakes and red sand islands.

2. When Lake Eyre floods pelicans fly in from all around Australia to breed on its islands.

3. Lake Eyre in flood is a rare and ethereal sight.

⭐ The hottest recorded temperature in the Australian desert in the last 100 years was 50.7°C (over 123°F) at Oodnadatta near the western edge of Lake Eyre.

DESERT FISH

When you think of deserts, fish are not the first things that come to mind but nearly every permanent waterhole or spring has at least one of Australia's 33 species of desert fish living in it. The most common – spangled perch, bony bream, desert goby and Lake Eyre hardyhead – are also found in temporary waterways and artificial bores. Only the hardiest can survive the wildly fluctuating desert conditions: pools that are tranquil most of the year can suddenly become raging torrents during rare storms, and shrinking, stagnant water-holes heat up in summer to unbearable temperatures while winter nights are often freezing. In winter many fish also become susceptible to gill parasites, which reduce their ability to extract oxygen from the water – in vain, they gulp for air as they succumb to the disease and become easy pickings for raptors and dingoes.

To add to all these problems numerous water birds feed on them and aquatic invertebrates thrive on their eggs and hatchlings. To counterbalance this high rate of mortality, many species produce hundreds of thousands of eggs to ensure that at least a few hatchlings survive to adulthood.

1

Despite the scarcity of permanent water, fish are able to persist for two reasons. Rarely do all the waterholes in a river system dry up at the same time; and flooding provides a means by which they can disperse. Permanent water-holes are the gene pools for Australia's desert fish. In them fish survive droughts and then explode into life whenever rain falls, rapidly multiplying and moving in the floodwaters to repopulate rivers and lakes in a remarkably short time.

Fish have extraordinary adaptations for desert existence. Almost all can live in salty water, but few can tolerate water saltier than sea water. However, the Lake Eyre hardyhead, whose marine ancestors colonized prehistoric inland seas, can live in water three times saltier than the sea. Most fish have ways of surviving poorly oxygenated water. Gobies

1. The spangled perch is one of the most adaptable fish in the centre. They are found in every river in the Lake Eyre basin and in most artesian pools.

2. The golden perch or yellowbelly is the centre's biggest freshwater fish. They produce thousands of eggs during floods.

300 eggs at a time, many thousands less than fish inhabiting ephemeral waterways. The male then takes the time to guard the eggs till hatching, ensuring more of his young survive.

Desert mound springs have a unique biological diversity due to their long isolation and special conditions. Dalhousie Springs boast six fish species, five of which are found nowhere else and have been isolated from other fish for around 10,000 years. Even shallow, marshy springs can have their own fauna – Edgbaston Springs, for example, has three endemic species, all with the smallest natural ranges of any fish in Australia.

Fish have an uncanny ability to find their way into farm dams and tanks. Many are undoubtedly pumped in either as eggs or as larvae, and wading birds may also be responsible for introducing eggs as they sometimes stick to their legs, but some fish have incredible dispersal ability. There are many stories of people finding fish in unusual places and claiming they must have 'come from the sky'.

However, in most cases they simply swam there. Spangled perch have been recorded swimming over 16 km (10 miles) in six hours along a wheel rut, stopping only because the water ceased flowing. Desert fish have a remarkable instinct to travel during and after rain. Even in the desert, rain can bucket down and form a sheet of water that fish can swim along. Once the rain stops, the water quickly disappears and the fish are left flapping. However, that story of 'raining fish' may not be as fanciful as it seems. Amazingly, they can be sucked up by whirlwinds and storms and, while most die during their airborne journey, some may fall back to Earth alive.

Compared to the world's other arid areas, central Australia's fish communities are in remarkably good condition. With the exception of a few keen anglers, most people don't even know that fish exist in the desert. They are surprised when they see them in waterholes and usually jump when a desert fish nibbles their toes.

will swim above algal beds in artesian springs, collecting oxygen given off by the algae. In emergencies many fish can even extract oxygen from the air, gulping it at the surface. However, desert fish are unable to escape shrinking waterholes and none produces eggs that are able to survive drying. Spangled perch and catfish are often found in the mud of drying pools but, while they have a remarkable ability to survive these adverse conditions, they will die if rain or floods do not eventually fill the waterhole.

Unlike the changeable desert streams, springs provide fish with a constant flow of water at much the same temperature and salinity. The most common fish in springs, the 6-cm (2¹/2-inch) long desert goby, shows a predictable evolutionary response to this stable environment – it produces fewer than

2

◆ TOPIC LINKS

2.3 Water in the Desert
p. 71 The Finke River

2.3 Water in the Desert
p. 76 Salt lakes

GUM TREE COUNTRY

OUT BUSH

This enormous continent supports a vast green wooded world, in some places remote and secretive, but elsewhere running right into the heart of cities. This is the great Australian bush.

Much of it is characterized by just one kind of tree – the eucalypt or gum tree. Capable of withstanding the drought, poor soils and violent fires that are a feature of Australia's landscape and climate, eucalypts pop up almost everywhere. There are over 700 species, and with a few exceptions in neighbouring islands, they are native to nowhere else in the world – they're true Aussies. They are found from the deserts of the centre to the edge of the rainforest, on snowy mountainsides and scorching rocky ledges. But their strongholds are the woodlands and forests that clothe Australia's outer edge. Here they are vital to a wealth of wildlife, including some of Australia's strangest and most charismatic animals, which live, feast and raise their young in gum tree country.

Previous page:
Eucalypts, or gum trees, grow almost all over the continent, sometimes as forests, sometimes as isolated trees, like these ghost gums growing near Alice Springs, in the centre.

1. Like many Australian animals, regent parrots rely on gum tree hollows to raise their young. These large and colourful birds usually are seen in pairs or small groups.

THE OLD GUM TREE

Stand in a eucalypt woodland in southern Australia on a summer afternoon and at first everything seems very quiet. The air is warm and the trees appear to droop, their long leaves hanging down and barely stirring. But gradually you begin to notice what's around. Kangaroos graze in the thin shade. You may see the fuzzy grey roundness of a koala high above, or make out the shape of an owl-like tawny frogmouth, looking like the branch it's sitting on. A bright parrot, a rosella, disappears into a tree hole, and a screaming party of pink galahs flies overhead. A kookaburra swoops from a branch and yells its unmistakable cackling call. The gum tree woodland is far from empty.

Gum trees are the essence of the Australian bush. These evergreen trees come in all shapes and sizes – the tallest flowering trees in the world are eucalypts; others are short and gnarled and grow in the snow. There are the ghost gums, their stark white trunks dramatic against the red rocks and dark blue sky of the hot centre, and the strange, multi-stemmed mallees that thrive in the very driest areas. All are recognizable by their drooping, grey-green leaves. At first sight these trees almost seem to be wilting in the heat. But the leaves hang downwards for a good reason – to avoid overheating in the sun's glare. Eucalypt woodlands are full of light and everywhere they grow there are animals around them.

Parrots eat eucalypt seed capsules, possums sip nectar from their flowers and

koalas chew their leaves. The holes these trees develop inside them are also major attractions to wildlife. More animals rely on tree hollows in Australia than in any other part of the world, and eucalypts are especially full of them. Watch for long enough and the chances are you will see an animal disappearing into the recesses of a gum tree.

Regent parrots and superb parrots are beauties of the southern eucalypt woodlands that flank the Murray River of southeastern Australia. These long-tailed parrots move out of the woodlands to feed on grass seeds, but build their nests in hollows inside the trunks of big old eucalypts, sometimes many metres down in the very depths of the cavity. Here the female lays her eggs and stays incubating them while the male goes out to

1. Grey kangaroos are grass eaters, sheltering in open woodlands in the heat of the day and coming out in the evening to feed.

2. Laughing kookaburras, with their unmistakable chuckling call and distinctive plumage, are very social birds, which often help to raise the offspring of their relatives.

1

gather food. Such an out-of-the-way nesting site provides protection from the elements and from marauding goanna lizards, which would happily make a meal of an egg or a chick.

Trees must reach a certain age before they start to form hollows. Over the years lightning strikes them, and bush fires, rain and wind ravage them. A tree can be perfectly healthy on the outside and continue to grow, while its inner wood is rotting and being eaten away by termites. A hollow big enough to house a parrot may take 200 years to form.

Watch at dusk and you might see a sugar glider emerge from its nest hollow to feed on insects and nectar up in the canopy. Smaller animals scoot in and out of smaller holes – tiny insect-feeding bats emerge from narrow cracks to hunt, and tree frogs creep out from shelters under the bark. One of the most intriguing animals to emerge from its gum tree home after dark is the antechinus. Antechinuses are small, mouse-like marsupials; speedy and nocturnal, they're hard to see as they forage around the leaf litter for insects. They build nests in tree hollows, but it's only the female that raises the young. After a frantic two-week mating frenzy in early spring, all the males die of exhaustion.

However, the classic hollow-nester is easy to see by daylight. The kookaburra is a dramatic-looking bird, nearly 50 cm (20 inches) long, with an impressive beak. When you see one out hunting, it may be feeding a nestful of chicks that don't belong to it. It may have reached breeding age itself, but there may not be sufficient resources available for it to start a family of its own, so instead it helps its parents rear their next brood, acting as a caring big brother or sister. Kookaburras often raise their young inside hollow eucalypts. Bold and familiar, they rank alongside koalas as the most characteristic inhabitants of gum tree country.

2

The didgeridoo, Australia's classic musical instrument, is made from a eucalypt branch that has been eaten hollow by termites.

NUMBATS – TERMITE GOURMETS

Australia is a country with vast numbers of termites. As a result there are plenty of animals that eat termites and one of the most intriguing is the numbat (right).

These exquisite little mammals, with their delicate build and striped fur, are unlike any other. Most of Australia's small marsupials are nocturnal, but the numbat is active during the day because that is when its food is available. Numbats are strictly termite-eaters and they feed when the ground warms up sufficiently for the termites to be active in their galleries under the leaf litter.

A feeding numbat is a remarkable sight: it sniffs and digs, turning over sticks and soil to expose termites in their shallow underground runs. Then it stretches out its long cylindrical tongue to mop up the feast. The tongue is sticky, and flicks in and out of the numbat's mouth with incredible speed. Numbats have teeth but they can't chew; they just swallow, getting through as many as 20,000 termites in a day.

Trees of the river

The most widespread eucalypt in Australia is the river red gum. Tall and stately, it grows near rivers, but it can survive even in the desert along salty watercourses that seem to have barely any water in them. This is an extremely tough tree.

Its principal stronghold is along the vast Murray River, where it forms beautiful woodlands of soft grey and green. The Murray itself is an Australian icon. It rises in the eastern highlands and doesn't hurry its 2500-km (1500-mile) journey to the Southern Ocean near Adelaide in South Australia, running wide and quiet through fertile farmland and semi-desert. All along its course grow river red gums.

One thing you notice in these riverside woodlands is the profusion of branches strewn across the ground. Eucalypts generally, and red gums in particular, have a disconcerting tendency to drop limbs without the slightest warning – not for nothing have they been called 'widow-makers'. Inside, the wood is rich red and so dense that if it lands in the river it sinks immediately.

Because of this, stretches of the Murray are full of 'snags', half-drowned fallen branches that are valuable to wildlife. Birds perch on them to drink, and turtles bask on them. They are also the perfect hideout for Australia's biggest freshwater fish, the Murray cod, which can reach 1 m (over 3 feet) long – even longer, if fishermen's tales are to be believed. Under these snags the cod can hide from predators, rest from the flow of the river and shelter from the sun. Each year these huge fish swim hundreds of kilometres upstream to mate and lay their eggs on submerged wood, but when they swim back downriver, they often return to exactly the same 'home snag' they left behind.

There is an event that happens every few years that might seem to be disastrous to the trees: the river rises unpredictably and spills over the low-lying land around it, flooding to a height of 1 m (over 3 feet). The woodland is awash, but far from injuring the trees, this is in fact what they've been waiting for. River red gums are not only flood-tolerant, they actually need to be flooded periodically so that their seeds can be carried off to colonize other ground.

If the flood is large enough the woodland is transformed into a wetland, where ducks nest in tree hollows, and egrets and cormorants, ibises and herons gather in the big trees to nest and breed and feed on the multiplying fish which swim around what was previously grassland. The trees themselves drink deeply and put on a spurt of growth. Big floods are rare these days, due to man-made changes in the flow of the mighty Murray, but when they do happen the results, for the wildlife at least, are welcome and spectacular.

★ A huge hollow gum tree in South Australia was home to a couple and their two children in the 1850s.

1. The Murray cod, Australia's biggest freshwater fish, uses fallen branches as shelter from river currents.

2. (opposite) Superb parrots are beauties of red-gum woodlands, They nest high in mature trees, and may travel many kilometres to forage on seeds.

Overleaf: When the mighty Murray River breaks its banks, the woodlands are transformed into wetlands and trees put on a spurt of growth.

1. Many eucalypts flower spectacularly and provide plenty of nectar. Insects, birds and mammals visit to take advantage of the feast.

2. Eucalypt flowers, like this Finke River mallee, unfold from often strangely shaped buds. 'Eucalypt' means 'well-covered': the developing flower pushes off the capsule lid that protects it.

THE FLOWERING OF AUSTRALIA

The Australian bush is an assembly of some of the most intriguing plants on Earth and some of the showiest. Although at first sight the colours of the bush may seem subdued, with tough leaves in hushed shades of greens and grey, this is a landscape full of vibrant flowers.

From the densest forests to the deserts, even the straggliest of eucalypts burst into bloom, with flowers that hang like curtain tassels. In some species they are small and modestly white or cream, but in others the blossoms are large and colourful, yellow or red or flame-orange, especially attractive to birds. The flowers are there for one reason only – to attract animals to collect their pollen and take it to other eucalypts, so pollinating them. In return the animals get a reward of nectar. Marsupials, bats and many birds and insects are all attracted by different flowers that appear through the seasons.

Flying foxes – large bats that like fruit – are also great nectar-feeders and may fly 50 km (30 miles) a night to find trees in flower. Rainbow lorikeets, one of Australia's most brilliantly coloured parrots, visit flowering trees in feeding flocks, lapping up the nectar with tongues shaped like little fringed mops.

Even in the most impoverished arid areas eucalypts attract animals to fetch and carry for them. In the dry mallee shrubland country of the south the gums grow as scrubby, bristling, gawky little trees, but in spring they too flower profusely. Tiny pygmy possums sleep in gum-leaf nests by day, and at night climb to the mallee eucalypts to sip from the flowers.

In the harsh, drier landscape of the centre, gum trees play second fiddle to the other classic flowering tree of the Australian bush, the acacia or wattle, which lights up the landscape in early spring with its bright yellow spikes or pom-poms of flowers.

2

Although the flowers have no nectar, they are much visited by insects, especially bees, which gather their protein-rich pollen. Acacias grow in other parts of the world, but Australia has more species than anywhere else and, like gum trees, here they are evergreen and have hard leaves which enable them to live economically in this tough country. Their seeds hang from bean-like pods and may simply pop out when the pod dries in the hot sun. The seeds are also helped to spread by emus, which eat them and later pass them out in their droppings, possibly even helping them to start germinating in the process.

The first European botanists in Australia were amazed by the sheer variety of flowers they found – huge banksias and grevilleas, orchids and featherflowers; in all there are over 20,000 native species, compared with 6000 or so in all of Europe. Many are unusual shapes: one of the most intriguing is the kangaroo paw, which looks just like its name and is pollinated by nectar-feeding birds such as honey-eaters. The flowers are shaped in such a way that as the bird perches and feeds, the pollen-carrying anthers bend forward and dab pollen on its head. When the bird visits the next kangaroo paw, the same thing occurs and so the pollen transfer is neatly made.

Part of the coast of Western Australia receives an average of about 10 hours of sunshine every day, making it one of the sunniest places on the planet.

Kangaroo paws are usually found growing in heathland, where the soils are extremely short of nutrients. No large trees grow here, but there is an astonishing variety of flowers. Walking through a patch of unspoilt coastal heathland is like walking in a garden. Everywhere your eyes rest, it seems, there's another flowering plant – some are tiny, some larger.

The southwest corner of Western Australia has vast areas of heathland, stretching along the coasts and on sand plains further inland, and it has one of the most diverse collections of flowering plants in the world. Many are found nowhere else in Australia, having been isolated for millions of years. During periods when the land went through arid phases the plants were marooned in tiny wetter refuges for so long that they could evolve into completely new species.

Here there is always something in bloom – vital for those animals that rely on the flowers for something to eat. Feeding on the banksias and grevilleas of these southwestern heaths, and living nowhere else, is the honey possum. This tiny marsupial, weighing only about 10 g ($^{1}/_{3}$ ounce), eats nothing but nectar and pollen, the only mammal in the world, apart from bats, to do this. It has a brush-tipped tongue, barely any teeth and a long, pointed snout to get inside the plants from which it sips. Very agile, it clambers around the flowers that dwarf it, using its fingers and toes to grip. The plants are vital to the honey possum, but then the honey possum is also important to the plants, carrying their pollen as it feeds. Plants and honey possum have evolved together, from the time when the rainforests still ruled the land and the true Aussie bush had yet to make an appearance.

2

1. (opposite) Dwarfed by the flowers on which they feed, honey possums eat only nectar and pollen. These tiny marsupials are mostly nocturnal, though they may occasionally be seen in daylight.

2. Kangaroo paws bear a strong resemblance to a kangaroo's feet and toes. Their strange shape helps the transfer of pollen to the heads of visiting birds.

 THE COMMUTING PARROT

Swift parrots (right) are smallish, bright green birds which, like many other parrots, feed on eucalypt nectar. But swift parrots are unusual because they travel a long way to find gum trees that suit their particular needs.

Tasmanian blue gums, eucalypts that grow on Tasmania's east coast, flower in the spring and Australia's entire population of swift parrots travels there to find them. The parrots time their breeding activity to coincide with the flowering of the trees and the subsequent abundance of blue-gum nectar, which is their main source of food during the nesting season. With breeding over and autumn on the way, most of the population heads off north to the mainland, flying fast and non-stop across the Bass Strait. Most spend the winter in southern Australia, following the various eucalypts as they flower, but some get as far as southern Queensland, 2000 km (1250 miles) away.

When spring returns they fly all the way back to Tasmania. Sadly, this little parrot is endangered, partly because its very specific breeding areas have been reduced by land clearance, and there may be only about 2000 birds left in the wild.

KOALAS

Koalas and eucalypts are inextricably linked in our imagination. It's one of the classic images of the bush: a chubby little bundle of grey fur up among the branches, munching away on gum leaves, often with a baby clinging on like an animated back-pack. With so many eucalypts and so many leaves to choose from it seems as if the koala has a relaxing time of it. All it needs to do is stretch out an arm and pluck another bunch.

1

2

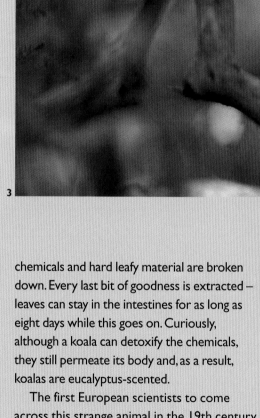

3

But it's not as simple as it sounds. Eucalypt leaves are not an easy meal – not only are they plastic-hard and low in protein, they are also full of poisonous chemicals strong enough to deter most browsers. Not many can survive on such a tricky, nutrient-poor diet. So how do koalas manage?

Their secret is a very effective digestive system, combined with lots of chewing and lots of sleep – with sleep being the most important factor. Koalas seem to do most things in slow motion. Watch one involved in almost any activity – eating, grooming, seeing off a rival – and within minutes it will have dozed off, virtually mid-action. They sleep 20 hours out of 24 but, by this strategy, they save enough energy from their meagre diet to keep them going for the other four.

A koala spends most of those remaining hours eating and has a number of ways of dealing with its food. It is selective about its choice of leaves, sniffing them first to check the chemical content. It's these chemicals that give eucalypts their distinctive smell. If they pass muster, the koala snaps off a twigful and starts to chew ... and chew ... and chew. It may also regurgitate and chew again, a little like a cow chewing the cud. When finally swallowed the leaves pass into the digestive system. Here they are processed in an extremely long, appendix-like chamber, the caecum, where toxic chemicals and hard leafy material are broken down. Every last bit of goodness is extracted – leaves can stay in the intestines for as long as eight days while this goes on. Curiously, although a koala can detoxify the chemicals, they still permeate its body and, as a result, koalas are eucalyptus-scented.

The first European scientists to come across this strange animal in the 19th century gave it a Latin name meaning 'ash-grey pouched bear', a reasonable mistake given its bear-like ears, long claws and big black nose. But a bear it isn't – it's a marsupial, which carries its developing young in a pouch.

teeth are well up to the job, but gradually, as it reaches middle age, its tooth enamel gets thin and then the softer dentine underneath begins to wear. Chewing becomes less efficient and so the ageing animal has to chew even more frequently to satisfy its energy needs. From then on it's a downward spiral – the teeth wear flatter and flatter, and finally the old koala is chewing up to 40,000 times a day and still not getting enough energy to keep it going. Eventually it just fades away, an otherwise healthy animal starving to death, its life-span determined by something as basic as the strength of its teeth.

However, a koala in its prime is a robust animal, superbly adapted to a life among the eucalypts, albeit a life lived by necessity at a very leisurely pace.

1. Koala young may stay with their mothers until they are a year old.

2. Koalas must come to the ground from time to time to move to new feeding trees.

3. The classic creature of the Australian bush, a koala's home is up a gum tree.

Slow to mature, the young koala remains in the pouch for about seven months, and even when it emerges it will stay with its mother until it's a year old. This means she may be carrying around an extra 25 per cent above her own body weight, another big drain on her energy resources. So she is forced to feed even more intensively to maintain her own strength. She must regularly move between trees to find the best leaves, a laborious process, given that gum trees tend to grow widely spaced and koalas are not very good at jumping.

Bottom-first, the koala mother clambers down to the ground, then makes her way on all fours through the understorey. She walks with the rolling gait of an animal not quite at home on the level, her baby clinging to her back like a child taking its first donkey ride. When she reaches the nearest suitable tree, she hauls herself and her baby up the trunk, using surprisingly long, strong limbs and grasping clawed hands to move to the upper branches, ready to feast – or perhaps have a nap.

Barring accidents and disease, a koala may live for 18 years, but it seems a lot is down to its diet. Eucalypt leaves are so tough they simply wear a koala's teeth out. A young animal may chew 16,000 times a day and its

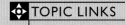 TOPIC LINKS

3.1 Out Bush
p. 83 The old gum tree

6.3 Last Refuges
p. 220 Kangaroo Island

THE HIGH COUNTRY

It may seem strange to think of Australia as having anything to do with deep snow and alpine wilderness. But in the southeastern corner there is a different landscape – extensive mountains.

Australia is the flattest continent on Earth, the result of millions of years of geological tranquillity. There is only one substantial area of highlands: the Great Dividing Range, a vast chain of raised land that runs the length of the eastern coast from Cape York in the north to Victoria in the south, re-emerging as the central highlands of Tasmania. The further south you go the higher the range becomes. But still, Australia's tallest peak is only a quarter of Everest's height.

Nonetheless these southern uplands, the Australian Alps, are full of surprises. Covered in snow for months of the year and with towering forests on their mid-slopes, they are home to plants and animals that are uniquely adapted to the unusual conditions.

1. Australia's alpine peaks, like Mount Loch in Victoria, are clothed in gum trees. Because this landscape is higher than the rest of the continent, the climate is colder and wetter than anywhere else.

LIFE AT THE TOP

Australia's mountains are not the jagged peaks of Europe or the Andes, or even of closer neighbours such as New Zealand. They are softer, more rounded, an indication of their great age: these are some of the oldest mountains in the world. Winters are beautiful, but conditions are demanding. If you live here you have to be prepared for bitter cold, icy gales and deep snow which can last for nine months of the year. Many animals pass through, but only the toughest can cope with the worst that nature has to throw at them.

Some unexpected animals brave the winter cold of the high country. Wombats have particularly soft, thick fur which insulates them from extreme temperatures.

In cold weather they forage during the day and can dig through 30 cm (12 inches) of snow to pull out a meal of leaves. Platypus also remain active all year, feeding comfortably even in icy mountain streams. Their secret is an outer covering of long, flattened 'guard hairs' that act like a drysuit, keeping their fine, dense underfur dry even during long periods underwater.

But perhaps the animal with the best survival strategy is the mountain pygmy possum. This tiny mammal lives nowhere else but the most exposed alpine uplands and it gets through the long winter months by hibernating, the only marsupial that does. Living here has its compensations, for the possum can take advantage of a seasonal feast that comes right to its door – thousands

of migrating bogong moths that fly up to the Alps to escape the heat of the lowland summer. Bogong moths spend this period among the high boulders, exactly where the mountain pygmy possums live, and so the possums have an easy supply of high-energy food. They rush to breed, the young growing quickly in the short summer, becoming independent at two months. Before the snow falls again the possum feeds up, rapidly doubling its weight, then rolls itself into a ball among the boulders, wraps its tail round its body and shuts down, its temperature dropping to just above freezing. There it stays for six months, with only fleeting intervals of activity, insulated against the worst of the weather by nothing except boulders and a thick blanket of snow.

1.Gang-gang cockatoos are often found in the highland forests of southeastern Australia. They have mastered the art of cracking open the eucalypt's hard seed cases, or gum-nuts.

2.Tree ferns, like these in Victoria, grow tall in wet southern forests, but they are dwarfed by the trees around them. Mountain ashes, majestic eucalypts, grow to 100 m (330 feet) – the tallest flowering trees in the world.

Snow gums

Mountain pygmy possums live above the point where trees can grow. The higher you climb, the more stunted the vegetation becomes as it struggles to survive in ferocious conditions. The trees that make it furthest are snow gums, cold-tolerant eucalypts which have the mountainsides to themselves. They are the only trees that can survive this high up and in the thick snows of winter they are a striking part of the alpine scenery. Fairly stately trees lower down the slopes, they become bent and twisted dwarves in the face of years of gales, their limbs pulled down by the weight of snow. They shed their bark in strips, and the colours revealed are beautiful – the gnarled trunks are flashes of bright red, pink and green. In the severest weather, their branches and leaves may be hung with icicles.

Snow gums provide valuable food for gang-gang cockatoos, which feast on the tree's seed capsules. These curious grey parrots are often heard before they're seen and their call sounds like a creaking gate. The males are the more conspicuous, with bright red heads and jaunty, Elvis-like crests of feathers. They eat noisily, cracking the hard gum-nuts and dropping the debris before moving on to the next tree.

But there comes a point when even the hardy snow gums can't survive – no tree can, because it is just too cold to keep its photo-synthetic engine running. So the highest ground is home to low-growing plants, which are blanketed by snow for much of the year, but which bloom spectacularly during the short spring and summer. Few plants can be as tough as the alpine marsh marigold, a beautiful scented flower which forms its buds during autumn and is ready to bloom early in spring – so early, it even flowers while it's still under the snow. It's a fabulous adaptation to a land where the winters are long and cold and the growing season is extremely short – only the fastest survive.

KINGS OF A MISTY FOREST

As you move down the mountainside, the landscape changes radically. On the lower slopes, at about 1200 m (4000 feet), are some of Australia's most spectacular forests. This is the land of the mountain ash.

Mountain ash thrives on southerly slopes where wet coastal air, forced to rise as it approaches the mountains, cools and dumps its moisture load. This wetness, and a fertility of soil thanks to ancient volcanic activity, make ideal growing conditions which are rare in Australia.

And these forests are wet – they receive 2 m (6 feet 6 inches) of rain a year. Walking through them in the early morning, when mist hangs like a veil, you feel almost saturated by greenness. Tropical-looking tree ferns tower 3 m (10 feet) above your head. Wattles and hazel form the lower canopy, along with myrtle beech and sassafras, remnants of the ancient rainforests that were here first. But these are all dwarfed by the real stars of the forest. British settlers who saw them first in the 1800s called them mountain ash, because they were homesick for the trees they'd left behind. They are actually eucalypts: *Eucalyptus regnans*, 'ruler of the forest'.

These trees are breathtakingly tall. Reaching 100 m (330 feet), and growing 1 m (over 3 feet) a year, they are the tallest hardwood trees in the world. Huge buttresses keep them up; their bark peels downwards in strips and hangs in streamers around the enormous trunk. They are so tall they can intercept moisture from clouds, and fog condenses on their leaves.

It's hard to see the animals, hidden in the dense forest greenery, but they're here. Occasionally, little swamp wallabies come out to browse during the day and wombats trundle about amongst the trees. You might get a fleeting glimpse of one before it vanishes **2** into its burrow among the roots again. Crimson rosellas, vivid red and blue and noisy, are more obvious and many smaller birds are visible too, some only seasonal visitors to the forest. Pink, flame and yellow robins flit through the lower foliage or pounce on insects on the ground. No relation to the European robin, they nonetheless have the same jaunty look and bright plumage.

Here, too, many animals are heard before they're seen. A noise like a rather loud, melodious whipcrack, ending with a 'choo-choo', is the call of the Eastern whipbird, but it's not just one bird that's singing. Males and females 'duet' across the forest, the male producing the 'crack' and the female the 'choo-choo', each half so precisely timed that it sounds like a single call.

The forest is full of different bird songs, but some of them turn out to be coming from one bird, the superb lyrebird. The male lyrebird is spectacular, with a lacy, train-like tail 70 cm (over 2 feet) long and a repertoire of songs that includes imitations of other forest

birds. He sings and uses his tail to attract females in an impressive courtship: he clears a number of stages for himself on the forest floor, scraping the bare soil into mounds, on which he struts about, singing and shimmering his tail over his head, until he draws the attention of a mate. He may sing for hours each day, this complex song possibly a way of communicating through dense undergrowth. Males mate with several different females during one breeding season, but for all his showing off he has nothing to do with the raising of his offspring. It's left to the female to build a nest and raise the single chick.

Possums in the trees

Many of the animals here are hard to see because they shelter by day inside the trees themselves. As they grow older, mountain ashes, like many gums, develop hollows inside their trunks and these provide homes for a multitude of wildlife. Most appear only when night falls.

There is one set of animals that is astonishingly adept at living among these trees. Watch a hole in a mountain ash after sunset and you might see a furry shape emerge and clamber around the branches or leap off into the darkness. Strange gurgles and grunts echo into the night. The possums and gliders are out and about.

Mountain-ash forests are home to a wide variety of species, from the tiny feather-tailed glider, the size of a mouse, to the cat-sized greater glider and mountain brush-tail possum. All have well-developed eyesight to help them find their way in the dark forest, and all have their own way of getting around.

Mountain brush-tail possums use hollows to sleep in, but they spend a lot of time foraging in the lower trees and on the ground, eating leaves and fruit and rooting around for fungi. Despite their chunky build, they are nonetheless accomplished climbers, moving down trees head-first and using their tails to help balance. Leadbeater's possum, smaller and much rarer, is another arboreal specialist,

1. Lyrebirds are spectacular inhabitants of mountain-ash forests. Males clear a 'stage' and put on an impressive song and dance routine to impress females.

2. Distinctive in their brilliant red and blue plumage, crimson rosellas are common in the tall forests and woodlands of the east, where they nest in tree hollows.

3. Some woodland marsupials, like this squirrel glider, have folds of skin that stretch between their limbs and help them glide between widely spaced trees.

dashing through the canopy and often leaping from branch to branch.

But the real acrobats are the gliders. The tiniest is the feather-tailed glider, at only 10 g ($^1/_3$ ounce) the world's smallest gliding mammal. Launching itself from a branch, it can achieve glides of 20 m (65 feet) and, when it is back in a tree, serrated pads on its feet help it get a grip.

All the gliders have membranes which stretch between their limbs and are spread out as they leap. The yellow-bellied glider, also known as the fluffy glider, can glide more than 120 m (400 feet). Coming in to land, it brings its limbs forward and hits the trunk with all four feet together, hardly pausing before it bounds on up the tree. It's an energy-efficient way of getting around for an animal that

weighs 700 g (1$^1/_2$ pounds) and eats only insects, nectar and sap. Its shrieking, bubbling call as it moves through the forest can be disconcerting in the darkness, but it's an important way for this highly social animal to stay in touch with others.

The largest of the gliding possums is the greater glider, weighing as much as 1.5 kg (3$^1/_2$ pounds). It dines almost exclusively on eucalypt leaves and, as a result of this low-energy diet, it's a slow mover, but it can glide 100 m (330 feet) and in flight can change direction by up to 90 degrees, using its long tail to steer. It spends most of its time in the canopy, as much as 80 m (250 feet) up. Sleeping in high hollows during the day and rarely coming to the ground, it's a real tree specialist.

The sooty owl, a secretive owl of the forests of eastern Australia, makes a call that sounds like a falling bomb.

THE TOP END

Australia is a land of contrasts. While the highlands of the south are deep in snow, the lands of the north crackle and bake during months of drought and fire. These are the northern tropics and here the Australian bush and the animals that live in it face a completely different set of challenges.

These 'wet-dry' tropics stretch across the top third of the continent, a Crocodile Dundee landscape that for half the year has virtually no rain. But then, in midsummer, spectacular storms come from the oceans to the north, and weeks of monsoon rains transform the land.

This again is a landscape dominated by gum trees, which thrive in a land so dry that, for much of the year, fire is an almost daily occurrence. But here the bush is also made up of other strange vegetation, around which live an astonishing diversity of animals, exquisitely adapted to a land that each year swings between desiccation and flood.

Previous page: Hanging Rock, in the Blue Mountains of New South Wales, overlooks a sea of eucalypts.

1. Jim Jim Falls in Kakadu becomes a torrent in the wet season; in the dry, it is barely a trickle.

FIRE AND FLOOD

The tropical north may seem a tricky place to live: many parts of it are remote; there are vast rocky gorges and escarpments; rivers full of crocodiles; fiery forests and watery plains; but here you will also find some of Australia's most stunning landscapes, full of drama and variation.

This warm, monsoonal land would be ideal for rainforest if it were not for the long dry season. Much of the Top End is clothed in eucalypts – this is another part of Australia where they took possession of the bush. The gum trees here are often widely spaced, many with bark that is rough and fibrous, earning them the common names of stringybark and woollybutt. In a place that sees no rain for five months and with a daily temperature reaching 30°C (86°F), these languid, pale-green, drooping trees look really at home, surrounded by tall spear grasses that grow quickly in the wet season, then go yellow and fall down in the dry months. The gums themselves, with their tough, water-conserving leaves and deep roots, are well able to survive the drought and they are surrounded by wildlife equally well adapted. Exquisite Gouldian finches nest in tree hollows and feed on the abundant grass seeds that drop in the dry season. At this time the eucalypts are spangled with white and flame-coloured blossoms, visited by lorikeets by day, and at night by clouds of flying foxes, which sip eucalypt nectar as well as feeding on fruit.

These northern forests are full of strange

The pygmy blue-tongue, a lizard of grassy woodlands, lives in trapdoor spider burrows, eating the original occupant first.

2

1. (opposite) Frilled lizards use their spectacular 'frills', large ruffs of skin, for display to deter rival males and attackers – but it's mostly bluff.

2. Northern quolls, with their distinctive brown and white spotted coats, are also known as northern native cats. They are feisty nocturnal hunters

animals that emerge only after dark. Quolls, kitten-sized mammals whose white-spotted bodies are camouflaged in the dappled moonlight of the woodland, come out from their den hollows to find food. These aggressive little carnivores hunt for insects, frogs, and small mammals. Northern quolls breed in the dry season: they're marsupials, but the female has a barely developed pouch and she carries her tiny babies around attached to her nipples. Rather more startling in the dark woodland is an animal whose call sounds like a soul in torment. The bush stone-curlew is a large, ground-dwelling bird that creeps around the bush at night looking for insects with its big yellow eyes.

As the dry season progresses, what appears to be cloud in the hot blue sky is really smoke. At this time of year this is a land full of tinder-dry dead foliage, and it burns at the slightest spark. Walk through a patch of woodland and the tang of smoke wafts in the air; ahead is a low-burning band of flames.

The fire front moves quickly, consuming the dead spear grass around the trees but also shinnying up the trunks of saplings and swallowing their leaves. Many little animals scurry out of the undergrowth to escape – skinks, grasshoppers and small mammals bolt from the flames and disappear into unburnt refuges. Within minutes of the smoke rising, the air is filled with birds. Whistling kites and falcons home in to feast on the easy prey laid bare by the flames.

One of the oddest inhabitants of these eucalypt woodlands escapes the burns by climbing the trees. Frilled lizards are unlike any other, nearly 1 m (3 feet) long and with a large ruff of skin around their neck that they raise for display. Approach one on the ground and it will hiss at you and extend its frill, but it's all bluff. In spite of their size and ferocious appearance, these are fairly timid insect-eaters. If scare tactics don't work, they will usually run away. Frilled lizards mostly run about on their back legs, with their bodies held upright,

heading for the nearest tree and bolting up it.

In the dry season frilled lizards spend 90 per cent of their time up gum trees, but they are much more visible when the wet season begins and one of their most important food sources appears. As huge thunderstorms boom over the woodlands, humidity rises and from the abundant termite mounds clouds of winged, breeding termites emerge to mate and begin new colonies. For frilled lizards this is a bonanza and they feast on the termites, putting on weight for their own imminent breeding season.

With the coming of the rains the woodlands take on a new vigour, the spear grass grows 3 m (10 feet) in three months, woodland pools fill with water and hundreds of frogs emerge to start breeding. In this driest of continents, this is one place where rain will always return, drenching monsoon rain that floods the landscape every summer and refreshes life parched by months of drought.

BURNING BUSH

Stroll in a eucalypt forest in southern Australia after summer rain and one thing you will notice is the smell. The scent of eucalypt oil is the evocation of the Australian bush; the blue haze that hangs over the tree-clad Blue Mountains outside Sydney is eucalypt oil in the air. The surprising thing is, one of the effects of this oil is that it seems to help the eucalypts burst into flames. Gum trees burn astonishingly easily.

No other continent burns so frequently and dramatically as Australia. This may seem like a catastrophe for everything that lives here, but the truth is rather more complex.

As Australia dried out many millions of years ago, the rainforest that clothed it in wetter times was gradually replaced by hard-leafed plants that could cope with the increasing drought and impoverished soil. Fire, sparked by lightning, became a key force and the eucalypts were able to survive it.

Then into this picture came people. Aborigines understood that burning the land would cause fresh foliage to grow and attract the grazing animals that could be hunted for meat. Over thousands of years, deliberate burning became commonplace. As a result of all these factors, the plants that could best cope with these taxing conditions thrived and, with their oily leaves and peeling bark, the opportunistic eucalypts were encouraging fire, to knock out the competition.

The eucalypt-rich lands of the tropical north burn most regularly, but these are 'cool' burns that barely affect the mature eucalypts, well armoured in specially thick, hard-to-burn bark. This is a land of rapid turnover. Fire cleans out the dead vegetation and clears the ground for new growth. Many fires are deliberately lit, to avoid a massive conflagration that would follow a build-up of years of tinder-dry leaves.

However, burns in southern forests are less frequent and more alarming. In a big southern eucalypt fire the temperature may rise to 1000°C (over 1800°F). The peeling bark acts like kindling, rising burning into the air and carrying the fire away to start another conflagration. The airy, leafy crowns burn like torches. Fire may even stay burning inside a hollow tree like a furnace, after the fire front itself has moved on. These are serious fires and the human cost can be enormous.

Many animals, of course, suffer after an intense fire, losing their homes and even their lives, but it's a subtle balance. Aboriginal hunters recognized that kangaroos and wallabies needed fire to stimulate the growth of new grass. The rare northern bettong, a small kangaroo-like animal that lives in the eucalypt forests of Queensland, relies heavily on fungi which may be stimulated to fruiting by fire.

Many Australian plants are adapted to fire. Banksias store their seeds in heavy-duty woody fruits that need an intense fire to open them up and release the contents, which the wind then carries away on papery wings. Grass trees send out their curious spiky flowers only after their shaggy heads

3

1. The frequent burns of northern Australia's eucalypt woodlands are a benefit to some animals – black kites chase insects flushed out of the vegetation by the flames.

2. Growing back: after fires, many eucalypts can resprout leaves from buds under their bark.

3. Grass trees grow for hundreds of years and survive many fires, their shaggy heads sprouting from the blackened trunk.

have been burned, and some acacias store their seeds in the soil, awaiting the time when a blaze will stimulate them to shoot.

The effects of fire in this fiery continent are diverse. Some eucalypts, like the mighty mountain ash, are killed outright by intense fires, but there's a twist. These trees can reproduce only by dropping seeds. The individual trees can't live forever; a 300-year-old tree is getting past its best. For its seeds to survive, it needs a clear space around it and a nutrient-rich bed for them to germinate. So when an old tree dies in a blaze, it leaves behind a bed of fertile ash that

will give its seedlings a head start. Without a fire at least every 300 years mountain ashes would not be able to regenerate and they would simply vanish under a succession of quite different plants. In fact, eucalypts and the ancient rainforest trees have been battling for supremacy, at least in the wetter parts of Australia, for millions of years. Rainforests can't survive fires of any intensity, while for eucalypts fire, if not too frequent, is a life force. If fire is kept out completely, the rainforest will push its way back, so fire is the key to which set of trees will win the battle for supremacy on their patch.

◆ TOPIC LINKS

3.3 The Top End
p. 105 Fire and flood

6.1 Human Footsteps
p. 193 Land of the Dreaming

KAKADU

It's early in the year and the Top End is awash. Water pours from rocks in huge waterfalls, rivers break their banks and spill out over the wide, flat land, but within a few months the rivers will have shrunk to pools and the flood-plains will be dry and cracking mud flats. How does the wildlife here cope with such transformations?

Everything in the Top End is under the influence of the weather. Though broadly divided between 'the dry' and 'the wet', the seasons pass through more subtle changes. Aborigines here recognize six seasons: there's the hot, deluging monsoon that starts in December and dumps well over 1 m (over 3 feet) of rain, ending when the storms start to clear in March; then come the cooler months of May and June, followed by the increasing desiccation of the early dry and hot dry seasons. In October humidity soars in the pre-monsoon period and spectacularly violent thunderstorms roll in; when the rains finally return, they transform the landscape.

Nowhere is this seasonal transformation more obvious than in Kakadu, a huge landscape of rock, river, forest and floodplain in the far north. Water birds in their thousands take advantage of the abundance of life that follows the wet season – and even in the dry there is always some water to be found. Hundreds of thousands of magpie geese are attracted to the area by the seeding of wild rice that follows the floods; they nest in the swamps as the water levels drop. Conspicuous by their highly domed heads, magpie geese have no relatives outside Australia and southern New Guinea. A male often mates with two or three females, who all lay their eggs in the same nest and share the duties of incubation.

Giant waterlilies grow luxuriantly and jacanas, long-legged water birds with enormous feet, stride about on the floating lily pads, feeding on insects and plants.

1

2

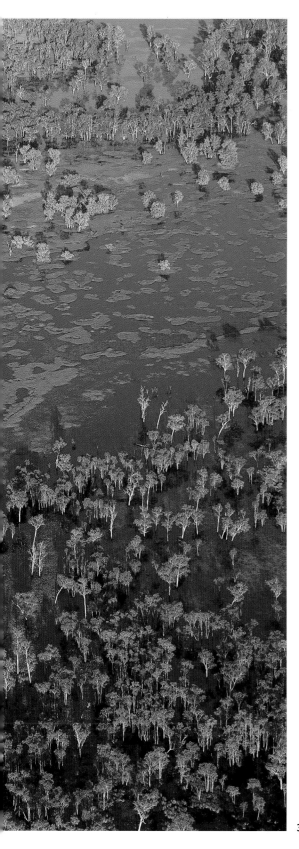

Unlike magpie geese, jacana males have the task of guarding the eggs on their watery nest and raising the chicks. The females leave straight after laying the eggs and look for another male to breed with.

The trees that do best in these wetlands are paperbarks, with trunks that look as if they're wrapped in thick wads of damp paper. You can float in a boat among these strange flooded woodlands, beautiful in the early dry when waterlilies and native hyacinths bloom. What looks like a floating log may be a semi-submerged saltwater crocodile. Despite the name, these crocodiles are quite at home in fresh water inland. Growing to 5 m (16 feet) and more, they're the world's largest reptile and very dangerous. Females nest during or just after the wet, building a mound of vegetation on which they lay 50 or so eggs, which they then cover and guard for three months. The babies squeak when they are about to hatch, the cue for the mother to open the nest and carry them out in her jaws to nearby water.

As the rainless weeks continue, the wetlands begin to shrink, forming isolated pools or billabongs. Water space is at a premium and gets increasingly crowded with water birds in spectacular numbers. Fish are trapped in the drying channels and birds take advantage of this concentrated feast – black-necked storks, one of the north's most dramatic-looking birds, wade around sweeping the water for prey with their huge beaks. Flocks of egrets and herons hunt by stabbing fish with their dagger-like bills; pelicans simply scoop up huge beakfuls.

But the going is getting tougher for everything. All life has to adapt to the increasing aridity as floodplains dry out. The long-necked turtle has a drastic way of surviving the dry – it feeds up well in the good times, then buries itself in the mud, which dries out and imprisons it, leaving it with only an air hole through which to breathe. Here it will stay, until the rains return and start the whole cycle going again.

1. Large and extremely dangerous, saltwater crocodiles are common inhabitants of the waterways of Northern Australia.

2. Paperbark trees, like these in Magela Creek, thrive in the extremes of Kakadu's wet and dry seasons.

3. A comb-crested jacana on its floating nest of lily leaves.

Overleaf: Pelicans in Kakadu. A feast awaits them as the water dries and fish crowd into shrinking pools.

1

THE KIMBERLEY, LAND OF ROCKS

In more ways than one, water has been the dominant force behind the landscapes of the tropical north. Eons of flooding rain have cut huge chasms in the rocky land, creating some of Australia's most spectacular terrain.

The Kimberley, in the far northwest, is a wide and remote landscape, three times the size of England. This is one of the oldest parts of the continent and some of its rocky ranges are the remains of an ancient reef, built 350 million years ago when large areas of this corner of Australia were under the ocean. When the seas receded, the limestone reef was left high and dry, to be dissected by millions of years of rainfall into deep gorges and caves.

Running through one of these ancient limestone ranges is the Fitzroy River, its floodwaters slicing their way over the millennia to form Geikie Gorge. On the walls of the gorge the water has exposed ancient marine fossils, the remains of long-extinct sea creatures that lived, died and were embedded here millions of years before the dinosaurs appeared.

The Fitzroy has sawfish and stingrays swimming in it, originally sea fishes that have adapted over 300 million years to a life in fresh water. It also has the curious archer fish which hangs around near the surface of the water, shooting down passing insects, or knocking them off overhanging vegetation, by spitting a jet of water at them. It does this by snapping its gills shut, and its accuracy is remarkable, especially as it has to allow for

the distorting effect of the water's surface.

At the height of the wet season the Fitzroy runs at a violent 27,300 cubic metres (nearly 1 million cubic feet) a second, surging halfway up the 30-m (100-foot) deep gorge, but in the dry months it's sluggish. The Lennard River, which has similarly thundered through the limestone reef to carve Windjana Gorge, doesn't flow at all in the dry, leaving its 100-m (330-foot) cliffs towering above pools of still water. These are inhabited by freshwater crocodiles, smaller and less ferocious than their saltwater relatives. They haul out to bask on the banks and increase in density as the pools dry. Though active during the day, they hunt at night for frogs and other small animals, sometimes lunging at the fruit bats that fly out at dusk to feed.

The riverbanks are lined with red gums,

1. The Fitzroy River cuts through the limestone ranges to form Geikie Gorge, in the Kimberley. The varying colour of the rock shows the level to which the river floods in the wet.

2. A boab tree in the Kimberley, with its distinctive barrel shape. In the dry season, these strange trees shed all their leaves.

paperbarks and native figs that make the most of any moisture that lingers here. But perhaps the strangest tree growing in the testing climate of the Kimberley's rocky ridges is the boab. This extraordinary, barrel-shaped tree can reach a girth size of 20 m (65 feet). In the dry months it sheds all its leaves, standing bare and odd, and when the rains return it bursts into bloom with large, creamy-white scented flowers, which are pollinated by hawkmoths. Found only in the Kimberley and the neighbouring edge of the Northern Territory, boabs are well adapted to drought, conserving water in their spongy wood, and they live for many years, possibly a thousand or more. In this ancient habitat, these ancient trees have seen vast numbers of wet and dry seasons pass by and survived them all.

TUNNEL OF BATS

In the strange landscape of the Kimberley's limestone country lie ancient cave systems, formed by the action of millions of years of rainwater. In the dry season it's possible to walk right through a water-worn tunnel running under the Napier range, in Tunnel Creek National Park. The tunnel runs for 750 m (2500 feet) and even in the dry season has deep pools of water in it. Stalactites hang from the roof, formed by the endless dripping of mineral-laden water. But there are other things hidden in the darkness.

Within these caves live at least five species of bat. Among these is the ghost bat, also known as the false vampire, unusual because it is Australia's only carnivorous bat. It roosts in the caves during the day and hunts at night for lizards, birds, insects and even small mammals, including other bats. It seeks out its prey with its big eyes and long ears and, embracing its victim with its wings, kills with a bite from strong jaws and carries it to a favourite feeding perch to devour. Large and pale, the ghost bat is found only in this and a few other areas of northern Australia.

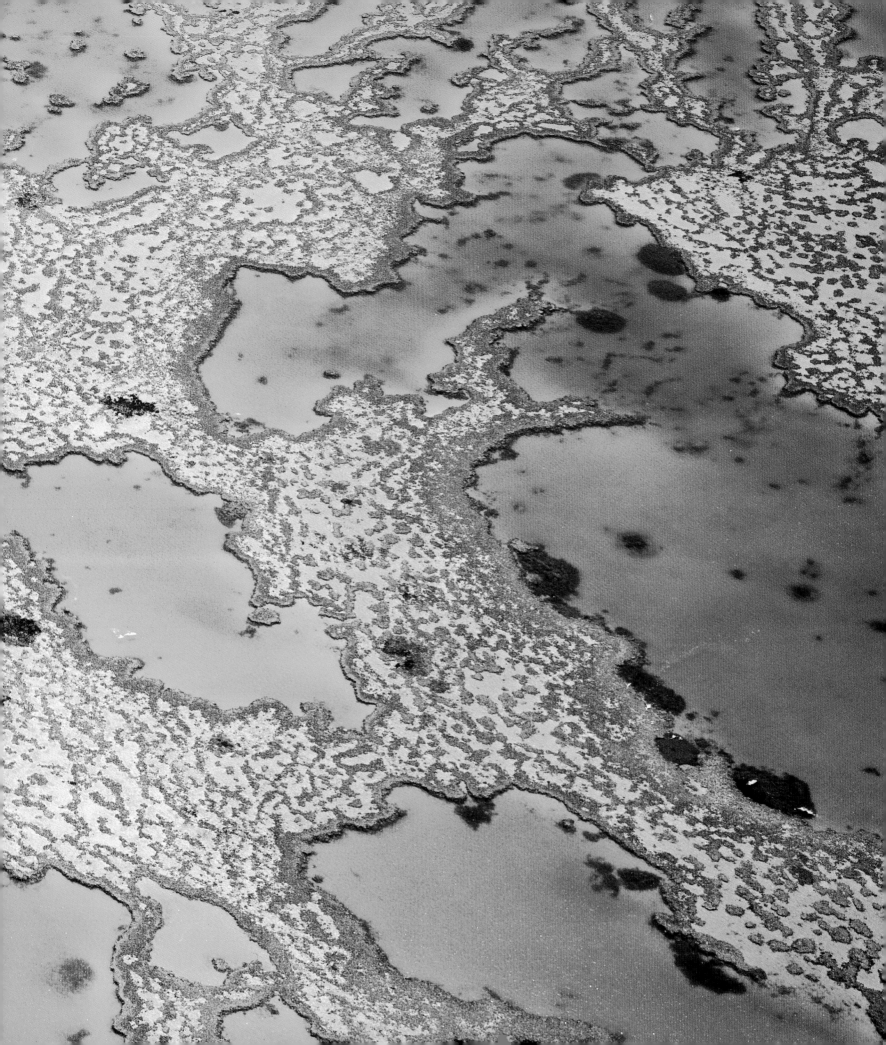

OCEANS

Australia is the world's only island continent. Its shores are bathed by the Pacific, Indian and Southern Oceans and stretch from the tropics to the Antarctic. Just as the land itself is largely arid, many of the seas around its coastline are also deserts, poor in the nutrients vital for life, and yet Australian waters support the greatest diversity of marine life in the world. The very top of the continent is a murky world of mud, a dynamic place with ferocious tides, but the warm, crystal-clear waters of the north also sustain two of the world's great coral reefs. Further south, the temperate seas are unlike anywhere else on the planet, inhabited by a cast of weird and wonderful marine creatures, many unique to the region. In the far south Australia is washed by the mighty Southern Ocean, the coldest and wildest on Earth, but also one of the most fertile, supporting incredible wildlife spectacles and pulsing life into the seas on the continent's southern margins.

Previous page: Corals thrive in the shallow protected lagoons on thousands of individual reefs that make up the Great Barrier Reef.

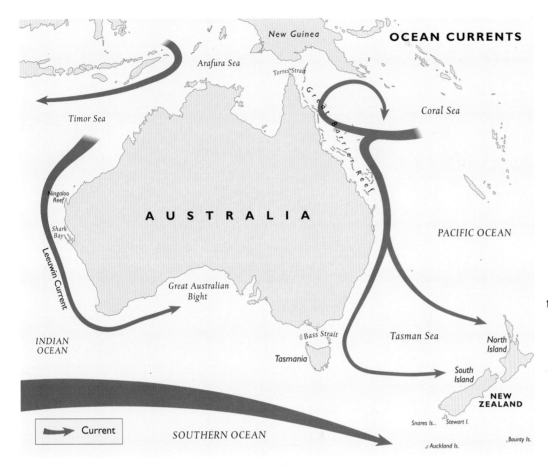

1. The tides in the Kimberley region are among the highest in the world and form a network of intricate drainage channels in the mud flats of King Sound.

WARM WATERS

Australia's tropical seas are a place of paradox. They are home to one of the greatest natural wonders in the world, the dazzling Great Barrier Reef, and also to Ningaloo Reef on the west coast, one of Australia's best kept secrets. However, the vast sea that stretches across the top of Australia between these two reefs is often dark and muddy, and frequently churned by massive tides. It could not be more different.

A world of mud

Northern Australia has a vast, remote coastline that meanders for thousands of kilometres from Cape York in the east to the Kimberley region in the west. This convoluted shoreline is fringed by large tracts of mangrove forests, fertile mud flats and endless sandy beaches. They may lack the colour and variety of coral reefs, but these murky tropical waters are full of surprises and are the most productive of the continent's tropical marine habitats. So how can these waters be so prolific?

The secret lies in the combination of shallow depths, huge tides and massive rivers. The Arafura and Timor Seas, which are bordered by northern Australia and the islands of New Guinea and Indonesia, are some of the shallowest seas in the world and lie within the monsoon belt of the tropics. A massive amount of rain drenches these regions every year and their swollen rivers pour nutrients from the land into the sea. These rich, shallow waters are then stirred into a thick soup by ferocious currents and phenomenal tides.

This area has some of the highest tides in the world and the biggest tidal range in the tropics. Near Derby the 12-m (40-foot) difference between high and low water produces awesome tidal spectacles. As the tide falls huge amounts of water rush through narrow coastal gorges and cascade off reefs to create churning rapids of sea water as powerful as any white-water river. The twice-daily ebb and flow of these tides has also created large areas of productive mangroves and mud flats along the length of the shore. With fertile margins and nutrients pumping into these waters from the land, all stirred by strong

1

tides and powered by the tropical sun, perhaps it is not surprising that the seas around the north of the continent are Australia's most productive, in terms of the sheer weight of life they support.

Roebuck Bay, near Broome in the northwest, contains the richest tidal mud flats in the world, providing a smorgasbord of small creatures for others to eat. More than 800,000 birds migrate here from as far away as the Arctic to feed on the vast areas of mud exposed at low tide. Over 300 species of bird have been recorded, more than a third of Australia's total. Fifty species of waders feed here and each has a differently shaped beak specially designed to feed on a different part of the assembly of worms, molluscs and crustaceans living in the mud. Mudskippers

proliferate in seemingly impossible concentrations, grazing the mud for as long as the tide will allow them. Battalions of golden ghost crabs also scour the surface for anything they can eat, from razor shells to sand eels, though they have to be wary of the local seagulls which prefer to steal food from them rather than find their own.

As the tide returns to reclaim these areas, a different cast of characters appears. Crabs and mudskippers take cover and the wading birds roost at the high-tide mark, whilst bizarre pop-eyed mullet and a multitude of sharks and rays move in. Pop-eyed mullet are small fish that thrive in their billions in this muddy world. They follow the rising tide, using their bifocal eyes to see both above and below the surface, useful when

keeping a look-out for predators that can come from land or sea. They dabble along in water barely deep enough to cover their bodies in an attempt to keep out of reach of the sharks. The aptly named shovel-nosed rays and prehistoric-looking sawfish sharks patrol these shallow waters and resort to extreme measures to catch the mullet. The sharks charge up the shore, actually beaching themselves in an effort to seize the fish, which explode from the water surface in a last-ditch attempt to escape. Gulls and pelicans gather to profit from the mayhem, and the sharks thrash around to launch themselves back into the sea, ready for another attack. Every turn of the tide triggers a new change along this remote and productive coastline.

2

1. Wind, waves and tide create beautiful patterns in the pure white sands of the Whitsunday Islands at the southern end of the Great Barrier Reef.

2. The blue-faced angelfish has a false eye spot near its tail to confuse would-be predators, making them strike at the wrong end.

Overleaf: Purple anthias feed on plankton in the water column but never venture far from their safe hiding place within the staghorn coral.

The Great Barrier Reef

Travel just a short distance down the east coast from Cape York and you arrive at the Great Barrier Reef, Australia's most famous natural wonder. From the air it is a visual masterpiece; the individual reefs appear to float like turquoise jewels in an otherwise empty ocean. Underwater it is a place of incredible beauty and variety.

This is the largest coral reef system in the world, stretching for an amazing 2300 km (1400 miles) along Australia's northeast coast. Its reefs are made up of over 400 species of coral, supporting well over 2000 different fish, 4000 species of molluscs and countless other invertebrates. Six of the world's seven species of marine turtle breed here and new creatures are being discovered

all the time. It is also Australia's most popular tourist attraction and, even though 2 million people visit each year, many reefs and islands remain largely unexplored because of the sheer size and complexity of the region. The Great Barrier Reef covers an area more extensive than Britain and is quite simply the largest living structure on the planet, and the only one visible from space.

It should really be named 'Great Barrier of Reefs', as it is not one long, solid structure but made up of nearly 3000 individual reefs and 1000 islands. Some of these are separated by just a stone's throw, others by many kilometres of open ocean. So how did such an immense living structure evolve? Coral has grown in this region for several million years but its modern form did not take shape ▷▷

⭐ A square metre (almost 11 square feet) of coral reef can manufacture 30 g (1 ounce) of limestone each day. This is eventually broken down into small grains which are washed up to form tropical beaches.

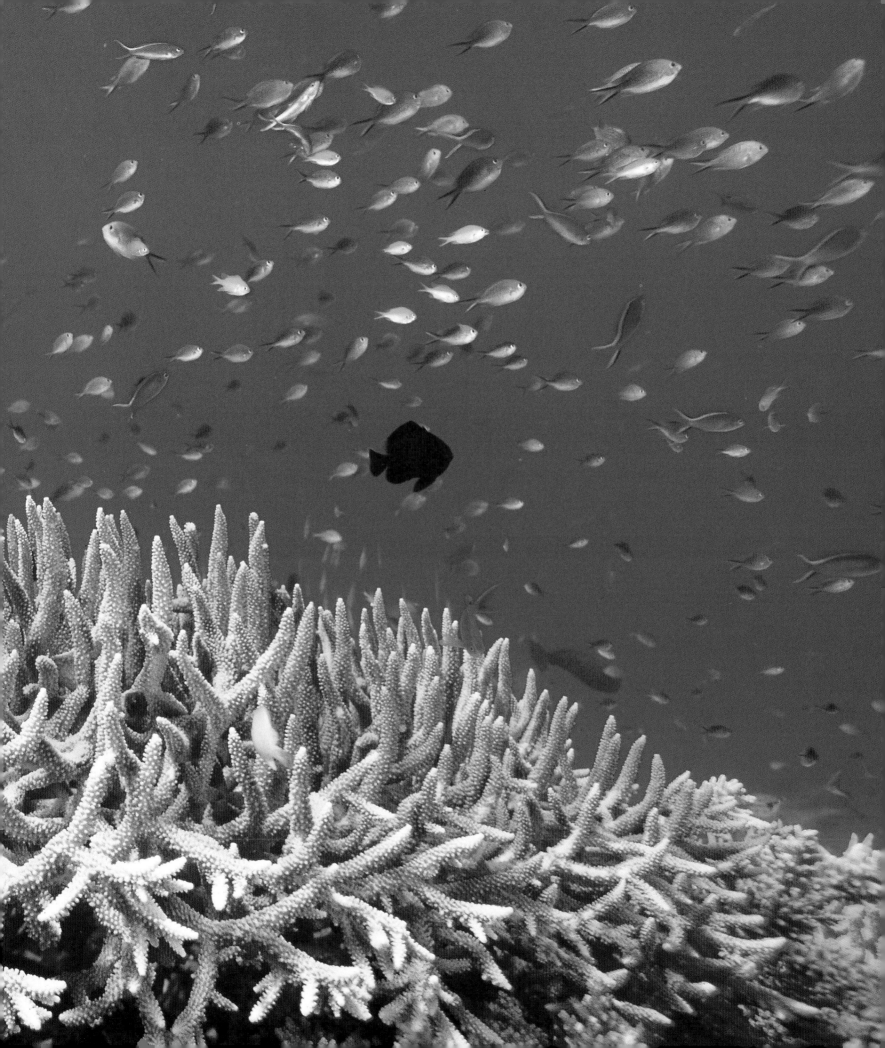

until after the last ice age. As the polar ice caps started to melt some 10,000 years ago, sea levels began to rise and the wide continental shelf of Australia was flooded. At the edge of that shelf corals grew and, keeping pace with the rising sea levels, they formed the Great Barrier Reef as we know it today.

Incredibly one tiny creature – the coral polyp – has built this vast structure. As single animals in isolation they look like a sea anemone, but most corals live in colonies. New polyps bud off the initial founder until colonies of thousands grow together, each connected to its neighbours by living tissue. One single lump of interconnected coral on the Great Barrier Reef weighs 15 tonnes and is made up of 30 million individuals. Hard corals build a limestone skeleton beneath their living tissue so that as coral colonies expand and grow whole reefs are formed.

Many visitors are surprised to find that the Great Barrier Reef is separated from the coast by a wide expanse of deep coastal water. Corals thrive only in clear water and so do not flourish in the murky near-shore waters of Queensland, but the continental shelf extends up to 160 km (100 miles) offshore where the shallow reefs are washed with clear oceanic water, creating the ideal conditions for corals. It is on this very outer edge of the continent that the best coral reefs are found, growing in an endless variety of plates and branches with a myriad of vivid colours and intricate shapes. This is one of the few places where you can see representatives of almost every animal group on the planet, and many you won't see anywhere else. Delicate butterfly fish explore every nook and cranny with their specialized mouths, while turtles glide through the azure water in search of coral cays to lay their eggs. Humpback whales

travel thousands of kilometres to calve in these clear waters while dainty little shrimps pick their way among the murk in the basement of coral city. Packs of white-tip reef sharks systematically patrol the reef front and sea birds wheel and dive in search of fish, while delicate flotillas of jellyfish float effortlessly in the current, dining on any small creatures that drift past. It seems that almost every way of making a living is practised here.

Not all of the Great Barrier Reef is the same – there is a huge variety of different reefs. Great Detached Reef in the north offers some of the best wilderness diving in the world, with fantastic visibility and steep drop-offs that attract superb pelagic fish such as sharks, trevally and barracuda. Raine Island, a remote coral cay also in the north, teems with wildlife above water as well as below, with thousands of breeding turtles and sea birds.

1

1. The vivid colour of this yellow boxfish is no bluff. In addition to its bony exterior it can also release poisonous mucous from its skin.

2. (opposite) This beautiful sea apple uses its feathery tentacles to trap food suspended in the water washing over the Great Barrier Reef.

The famous Cod Hole, on the sloping table of a reef near Lizard Island, is home to the gentle potato cod, an enormous fish the size of a family car but tame enough to swim between the legs of a diver. Further south, swirling patterns formed by the ever-moving sands of the Whitsunday Islands create works of art in the ocean, bordered by beautiful beaches and rainforest. The variety is almost endless.

But what drives this extravagance of colour and activity? How is such biological wealth even possible when these clear blue tropical seas lack abundant nutrients and plankton, the very basis of the food chain? In these waters virtually all of the animals living on the reef ultimately rely on the ability of plants to convert solar energy into food and body-building materials. The secret of the Great Barrier Reef's productivity is that many of the plants live inside the polyps. Corals harbour microscopic algae called zooxanthellae and these synthesize the sunlight and waste products of the polyp into oxygen and food substances, which leak into the tissues of the polyp. Corals get up to 98 per cent of their nourishment from these algae, so if it weren't for this special partnership very little would survive in these infertile waters – the corals themselves are the basis of nearly all life here. It is a paradox that something as colossal as the Great Barrier Reef owes its existence to microscopic algae and tiny coral polyps.

Ningaloo Reef

Though less well known than its famous east-coast cousin, Ningaloo Reef is remarkable and unique in its own way, hugging the arid west coast for over 260 km (160 miles), which makes it the world's longest fringing reef. Hardly any rain falls on this desert shore, so the inshore waters are crystal clear and corals thrive right up to the land. They grow in extensive lagoons protected by the outer reefs which, in some places, are as close as 100 m (330 feet) to shore. It's a fabulous place for snorkelling, as you can be over a coral reef within seconds of leaving the beach. An idyllic place called Coral Bay is one of the most

1

accessible and swimming here, through shoals of shimmering fish and over the gardens of colourful staghorn corals, is like being immersed in a living aquarium.

Coral reefs are famous for their fish life and Ningaloo is no exception. An unbelievable variety lives among the coral city and each species uses the reef in a slightly different way. Some, like the beautiful angelfish, delicately pick at the coral polyps, whilst the colourful parrotfish crunch off great chunks. Whole reefs are cloaked in thousands of golden cardinal fish picking plankton from the current and rolling curtains of juvenile striped catfish scour the sand flats surrounding the reef.

2

1. The tiny yellow dots covering the tentacles of these *Tubastraea* corals contain stinging cells to catch small animals drifting on the current.

2. The corals of Ningaloo Reef grow right next to the desert coast, unlike the Great Barrier Reef which is up to 200 km (120 miles) offshore.

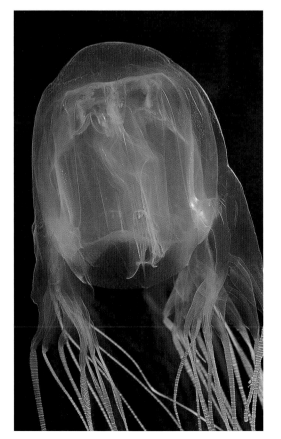

 MARINE NASTIES

Australia is known for venomous, biting and stinging wildlife on land, and the seas are no different. Sharks and crocodiles may grab the headlines, but when it comes to dangerous Australians it is the smaller marine creatures that hurt and kill more people. Top of the list is the box jellyfish (left), the world's most dangerous jellyfish. Over the past century they have killed over 70 people, more than the toll for sharks and crocodiles combined. They are so venomous that victims may be dead within just four minutes of being stung. These ghostly killers trail a mass of tentacles, each up to 5 m (16 feet) long, which are packed with millions of highly venomous stinging cells. They're designed to snare small fish, but people who are stung by this deadly jelly suffer excruciating pain.

The blue-ringed octopus is a beautiful creature, but one bite can kill a child. These little cephalopods are not aggressive and when disturbed produce an unmistakable alarm signal of vivid blue rings. They press home their attack only if victims ignore this distinctive warning.

Cone shells live in the shallows of most coral reef-tops and hunt fish by shooting out a venomous dart, rapidly paralyzing their prey. At first sight the beautiful shell may look empty, but it is not advisable to go near these deadly animals. Their dart contains a powerful cocktail of neuro-toxins which can kill a person within hours.

Bottlenose dolphins have such acute echolocation that they can detect an object the size of a ping-pong ball over 100 m (330 feet) away.

1

1. Whale sharks, the biggest fish in the sea, gather at Ningaloo every autumn to feed on the rich plankton bloom fuelled by the reef.

2. (opposite) The seasonal flush of life also supports immense schools of anchovies, visible as a dark slick in the shallows. Predatory sharks hunt along the edge of the shoal.

Ningaloo Reef is famous for one particular seasonal visitor, the whale shark. These are the biggest sharks in the world and the largest fish in the sea. They come to Ningaloo between March and May every year, and this is one of the few places in the world where whale sharks gather in large numbers so close to shore. So what draws them there?

Much of the energy produced by the creatures of Ningaloo Reef spills into the surrounding sea, fertilizing the waters and fuelling a rich plankton bloom. It is on this tiny planktonic prey that the whale sharks feed. They can grow up to 12 m (40 feet) long, with mouths up to 1.5 m (5 feet) wide, and yet they feed only on miniature animals. They effort-lessly filter millions of litres of sea water with their massive mouths, consuming anything

from tropical krill to microscopic plankton.

Whale sharks themselves are a mobile habitat for other creatures, attracting a host of ramoras and other sucker fish which cling to their tough sandpaper skin, whilst shoals of young trevally swim in the pressure wave created in front of the shark. Tourists flock here at this time of year to catch a glimpse of a whale shark; swimming with these huge animals is a breathtaking experience which few ever forget. However, very little is known about them. The majority of sharks gathering here are immature males, ruling out the possibility that this is a mating aggregation, so why are they here together? Where do they go for the rest of the year? Where and when do they breed and pup? What are their migratory routes? All these questions remain to be answered.

SHARK BAY

Imagine a bay where dolphins glide through calm turquoise water, ancient life forms still flourish and mermaids cruise gently through underwater meadows. This isn't an imaginary place, it's Shark Bay on the most westerly point of Australia. What is even more surprising is that all this life prospers in water that is extraordinarily salty, even for sea water.

Shark Bay is almost completely enclosed by a parched desert shore, so hardly any fresh water flows from the land, and little sea water flushes in from the open ocean. With only limited water movement within the bay, the fierce sun and a gentle breeze create ideal conditions for evaporation. This means the sea water is much more salty than normal, especially in the inner reaches of the bay. This high and varied salinity is the key to the unique collection of life here. The briny conditions exclude less tolerant plants and animals, which would otherwise be potential competitors for those that remain.

Seaweed, which would normally cloak the sea bed, cannot survive in these salty waters; instead, the sandy bottom is covered in pastures of sea grass. Unlike seaweeds, which are primitive algae, sea grasses are flowering plants just like their relatives, the familiar grasses on land. The average depth of Shark Bay is only 10 m (33 feet), so the sun easily penetrates to the bottom, lighting and warming the clear water and fuelling the growth of the millions of gently undulating fronds.

Sea grass is the foundation of most of the life of Shark Bay. Unhindered by choking weed, these aquatic grasslands cover 4000 sq. km

(1500 square miles) – nearly a third of the bay. That makes this the largest area of sea grass anywhere in the world. The community that inhabits these pastures is as diverse and fascinating as any coral reef and includes psychedelic sea slugs, cryptic crabs and bizarre fish, all toiling away and largely hidden among the fronds. These pastures are also where mermaids roam. The 'mermaids' are in fact dugongs, giant marine herbivores once mistaken for mythical beauties by sailors who had been too long at sea.

Dugongs, also rather appropriately called sea cows, spend up to eight hours a day grazing the underwater pastures. These languid creatures could hardly be described as beautiful, but they do have a certain portly grace underwater, as well as a surprising turn of speed. This is critical for avoiding tiger sharks, swift predators that live here in greater numbers than almost anywhere else in the world – it is not surprising that the bay was named after them. The tiger sharks have plenty of food available, apart from dugong. Their prey includes sea snakes, turtles and dolphins. About 3000 bottlenose dolphins live in Shark Bay and many of them have scars from shark attacks.

Some of the dolphins here have become world famous. At a place called Monkey Mia a few individuals have learnt that if they come to the beach at certain times, they'll get a free

3

1. Shark Bay is home to the largest population of dugongs in the world. As many as 10,000 of these gentle creatures graze the submarine sea grass pastures.

2. These domes of limestone are stromatolites – living rocks built up by microbes over thousands of years.

3. Bottlenose dolphins have excellent vision and use sight as well as echolocation to hunt fish among the sea grass.

fish. The arrangement, which started back in the 1960s thanks to fishermen who tossed unwanted fish to passing dolphins, now attracts 100,000 tourists to this remote outpost of Western Australia every year. All the other dolphins in the bay catch their own food, using their sonar to search the underwater prairies for fish hidden in the grass or under the sand.

Most of the creatures in Shark Bay, like the dolphins, ultimately depend on the sea grass which thrives here. But in some parts of the bay the salty conditions are even more extreme. In a few coves, such as Hamelin Pool, the water is too salty even for sea grass. But some plants and animals relish this tough environment. Swarms of jellyfish pulse up and down in the clear water, as algae living in their watery tissues soak up the sun. The sea floor is also covered with millions upon millions of tiny clams. Unchecked by predators which can't survive in the salty water, these molluscs

have been proliferating for thousands of years. Through time, storms have piled their delicate shells into huge beaches which stretch for many kilometres and extend inland for hundreds of metres. These beaches are a brilliant white and made of pure seashell.

However, there is something even more remarkable in Hamelin Pool – living fossils which have remained unchanged in form for over 3 billion years. Stromatolites may look like concrete pillars, but they are alive. They are formed by filaments of microscopic bluegreen algae which trap sediment particles as they grow. This builds up a pillar on top of which the living algae grow. These ancient plants are slow growers and add just a millimetre or so of sediment per year, which makes the 1-m (3-foot) high domes about 1000 years old. The unique conditions of Shark Bay mean it is one of the few places on Earth where stromatolites still survive.

 TOPIC LINKS

4.1 Tropical Seas
p. 126 Ningaloo Reef

4.2 Temperate Waters
p. 133 The Leeuwin Current

TEMPERATE WATERS

Travel south of Ningaloo or the Great Barrier Reef and you enter cooler, temperate waters that at first appear less colourful and vibrant than the tropical reefs. Neither do they support the immense numbers of fish, birds and marine mammals that characterize the cool waters of many other continents. Instead, Australia's temperate seas have produced an incredible diversity of unique plants and animals, many found nowhere else on the planet. Cathedral-like forests of giant kelp proliferate and create under-water jungles that are as awe-inspiring as the rainforests on land. Extensive kelp gardens provide ideal habitats for some of the strangest creatures in the sea. Cryptic sea dragons flutter in and out of the fronds and giant cuttlefish mesmerize their prey with fantastic light displays. Even the sea lions inhabiting this coastline are different from other seals. The extraordinary wildlife in these seas is partly due to a very unusual ocean current.

THE LEEUWIN CURRENT

On the west coast of Australia a warm-water current flows south from the tropics, past Ningaloo and down to Perth, eventually turning the corner of the continent into the Great Australian Bight. Travelling at about 100 km (60 miles) a day, it has a profound impact on the marine life of these shores. Its warm waters enable the world's largest population of dugongs to feed year-round in Shark Bay, the southern limit of their range. The Leeuwin Current also disperses tropical fish and invertebrates southwards into temperate waters, taking corals as far south as Perth. But this surface current also has a negative effect, preventing cooler, nutrient-rich water from welling up from the deep, making these some of the least fertile seas in the world. However, that in turn has encouraged many strange animals and unique solutions to surviving in a place where food is in such short supply.

Great Australian Bight

The arc of the Great Australian Bight is literally like a 'bite' taken out of the southern shore of Australia. It is bounded by an unbroken line of cliffs where the flat and featureless Nullarbor Plain plunges dramatically into the Southern Ocean. This huge area has a wide continental shelf and abundant sunlight, yet lacks the immense numbers of fish, birds and mammals that characterize other temperate seas. In addition to the effect

1. The waters around Australia's southern coast are unusually clear because they lack the dense plankton community that reduces the visibility in other temperate seas.

1

of the Leeuwin Current, the rainfall in southern Australia is so minimal that few nutrients flow from land to sea. Incessant breakers pound the sheer limestone walls of the cliffs and make life difficult at the surface, but beneath the turbulent waves sunlight illuminates forests of colourful seaweeds. Without the nutrients to support a dense community of phytoplankton, the water in the Great Australian Bight lacks the green tinge of most temperate seas, so the sun's rays can shaft through the clear water and penetrate deep down to the sea floor. This allows bottom-living plants to dominate the flora; a diverse community of seaweeds flourishes, which in turn provides food and shelter for an assortment of weird fish and colourful invertebrates.

Just as on land, isolation has had a profound influence on Australia's marine life. These shallow southern seas have been separated from other coastal waters by vast tracts of open ocean, as much a barrier to some marine life as they have been to Australia's terrestrial wildlife. The result is a multitude of specialist animals. Australia's temperate seas have some of the highest levels of species-diversity in the world and 90 per cent of the fish, molluscs and echinoderms living here are found nowhere else.

Sea dragons and walking fish

Magical sea dragons drift amongst the enchanted underwater forests of the Great Australian Bight and bizarre walking fish perambulate along the sea floor between stands of Tasmanian kelp. Australia's temperate waters are home to creatures that are so weird they might as well be from another world.

The weedy and the leafy sea dragons are related to sea horses and pipe fish, but are far more spectacular. The weedy sea dragon is coated with iridescent blue stripes, orange and pink bands and thousands of yellow polka dots. Despite its vivid colours it is not easy to spot underwater, even though it can be up to 45 cm (18 inches) from snout to tail. The dazzling patterns actually seem to work like camouflage in the dappled and tangled world of the weed. However, there is another species which has even more flamboyant appendages and is even better hidden.

1. The Bunda cliffs mark an abrupt end to the flat plateau of the Nullarbor Plain. The sheer limestone rock face stretches for over 200 km (120 miles), unbroken by inlet, estuary or river.

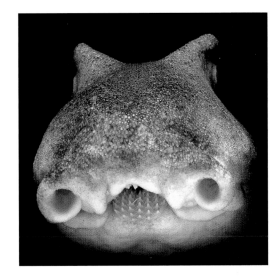

 ## SHARK SEAS

The incredible diversity of marine habitats around the continent supports a bewildering array of sharks – over 150 species, from the infamous great white to the bizarre-looking Port Jackson shark (left) and wobbegongs. Great white sharks, also known as white pointers, hunt fish, sea lions and fur seals around Australia's temperate coast, but are rarely glimpsed by people. In fact, grey nurse sharks are the only large sharks seen regularly on the coastal reefs of southern Australia. They cruise along with mouths agape, exposing long and apparently menacing teeth. They were once persecuted as man-eaters because of their fearsome appearance, but are now considered harmless unless antagonized.

Wobbegongs, on the other hand, are reputed to be the worst-tempered sharks in the sea. 'Wobbies' may appear lazy, but they move like lightning after food or the hand of a harassing diver, and their teeth can inflict a painful wound. Although there have been no fatalities, more divers in Australia have been bitten by wobbegongs than any other shark.

1

The strange leafy sea dragon appears almost unreal, with elaborate fins that seem draped with hanging foliage. But why do these fish go to such lengths to stay hidden?

In common with sea horses, dragons have a bony skeleton which offers little protection from their main predators, sharks and rays. Their only defence is camouflage and they blend in with the seaweeds of their local environment so well that most predators – as well as scuba divers – can pass close without noticing them. Leafy sea dragons drift with the tide and sway with the surge, making them almost impossible to spot among the waving fronds. Such excellent camouflage also comes in handy for stalking prey. Like chameleons, the dragons have independently roving eyes which help to pinpoint their minute quarry. The prolonged snout is used like a pipette to suck up mysids, tiny shrimp-like crustaceans. Dragons can hover incognito among a

1. The leafy sea dragon has such elaborate appendages that it can't swim very fast, but instead tends to drift with the surge.

2. The sargassum anglerfish uses its large extendable mouth to suck up unsuspecting prey in a fraction of a second.

☆ Australia has recorded more shark attacks than any other country, but this is still fewer than the number of people who are killed by bees every year.

buzzing mysid cloud, picking them off at will with hardly a visible movement.

Dragons are not the only strange fish in these cool waters. Handfish are aptly named, as their pectoral fins resemble hands, enabling them to 'walk' rather than swim. They also feed on mysids, using distinctive lures on their heads to entice prey closer to their gargantuan mouths. They are equipped with some of the fastest jaws in the sea, and can swallow whole swarms quicker than the blink of an eye.

Handfish and dragons have ingenious ways of ensuring their young get the best possible start. A pair of dragons shares the responsibility of rearing their offspring, for the male incubates the brood on the outside of his body. When the female is ready to lay her eggs, she extrudes them as a long sheet and presses them onto the male's body with her belly, although how they manage this

with all those elaborate appendages is anyone's guess. Each of the 300 or so eggs is partly embedded in the male's skin, where it develops and grows for about two months until it is ready to hatch. This long incubation means that sea dragons usually have only one brood each summer. The babies emerge over a period of about six days and their yolk sacs then support them for the few days it takes for their snouts to grow long enough to enable them to feed.

Handfish are equally attentive parents. Females wrap their egg mass around fixed structures such as algae, sea grasses or sponges, in a process which may take several hours. They then guard the fertilized eggs for seven or eight weeks until the young hatch. Baby handfish emerge as fully formed juveniles just 6 mm ($^1/_4$ inch) long. They drop to the reef and simply 'walk' away.

2

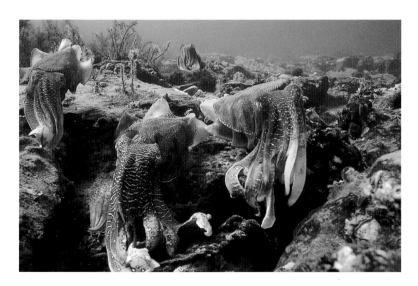

 GIANT CUTTLEFISH

The Australian giant cuttlefish (left) is the largest of the world's 100 or so species of cuttlefish; it can grow to lengths of 1.5 m (5 feet) and weigh nearly 15 kg (33 pounds). These colourful cephalopods aggregate in their millions along the south Australian coast every autumn. Giant cuttlefish need a hard substrate on which to lay their eggs, so they gather on rocky reefs to breed. The cuttlefish hover like alien spacecraft, constantly bickering as they bump into one another in the dense gathering. Males duel using an intricate combination of colour and body language, pulsing vivid stripes of blues, purples and greens over their mantles. Groups of up to seven huge males battle with each other using intense blasts of colour until one emerges as the winner. He then turns his attentions to the smaller females, mesmerizing them with another kaleidoscopic display. After mating, a female will lay about 200 golfball-size eggs among crevices in the reef, which hatch into miniature adults several months later. These tiny creatures go on to live and grow for two or three years, longer than any other species of cuttlefish, which is perhaps why giant cuttlefish grow to such an immense size.

Underwater jungles

Australia's southern coasts are dominated by extensive submarine forests of kelp. The elaborate fronds of these seaweeds are often intensely coloured and range from vivid emerald green to iridescent burgundy. As plants they manufacture living tissue from the sun's energy and are the beginning of the food chain. As with corals on tropical reefs, kelps provide a haven for fish and invertebrates from where they can search for food, raise their young and hide from enemies. Blue grouper wrasse cruise through the forests hunting for sea urchins, using their thickened lips to devour the prickly mouthfuls. The striped old wife fish, usually seen around the kelp in small groups, was given its curious name because of the grating sound it makes when stressed. Below the kelp a carpet of multi-coloured starfish and sponges appears for brief moments when the kelp fronds part in the current.

How is it that such magnificent plants can survive in waters which lack the nourishment to support even tiny phytoplankton? These large seaweeds can store nutrients in their fleshy tissue, enabling them to capitalize on the occasional influx of nourishment. Many also have ridges and spikes on their fronds to increase the surface area over which they can absorb food. Light easily penetrates through the clear water, allowing the kelp to photosynthesize even at depth, so they can grow well on the sea floor, which they carpet with a thick layer of vegetation throughout Australia's cool coastal seas.

The seaweeds of Australia have evolved in isolation, just like the sea dragons and handfish. So, of the 1000 or so species in these waters, more than 70 per cent are unique to the region and this southern coastline supports one of the most diverse marine floras in the world.

The common kelp is found on rocky reefs throughout Australia's temperate coast, from Western Australia to Queensland, and is probably the most abundant seaweed of any kind. The 1-m (3-foot) long plants form a dense canopy over a growth of encrusting red algae and smaller seaweeds, providing shelter and food for many creatures such as abalone and lobsters. There is also a microscopic community of exquisite animals living on the leathery fronds. Intricate colonies of bryozoans and hydroids emerge from their silicone shelter to comb the water for food.

Of all the seaweeds here, the most impressive are the magnificent, cathedral-like forests of giant kelp. Anchored to the sea floor by massive spaghetti-like holdfasts, these immense plants grow from a depth of 25 m (80 feet). Once they have reached the sunlit surface they continue to grow as much as 60 cm (2 feet) a day, making giant kelp one of the fastest-growing plants in the world. These forests are stunningly beautiful. Chinks of sunlight pierce the undulating fronds, penetrating deep down through the gin-clear water. Disguised among these plants are big-bellied sea horses and weedy sea dragons which occasionally break cover to flutter from one plant to the next. Giant kelp forests are limited to a few small areas around Tasmania's southeast coast, beyond the reach of the Leeuwin Current, but washed by the cool, nutrient-rich waters of the Southern Ocean.

 FISH FARMERS

The shallow reefs around Rottnest Island near Perth are covered with bizarre patterns which baffled people for years. From the cliffs they appear like a mosaic of polygons, but underwater they are in fact hedgerows of tall seaweed surrounding meadows of short algal turf. The cause of these weird shapes is a fish farmer — not a person who farms fish, but a fish that 'farms' algal turf. Each of the 6-m (20-foot) wide polygons is occupied by a single large fish, a western buffalo bream, which feeds on the short algae. They maintain their 'garden' by weeding out the large unpalatable seaweeds that reduce light penetration to their favoured plants. Each resident fish patrols its territory borders, stopping occasionally to threaten its neighbour and this aggressive posturing prevents both fish from weeding a narrow strip between the territories, creating a 'no man's land' where the distasteful seaweeds grow into tall hedgerows.

1. (opposite) Branches of giant kelp stretch to the surface, buoyed by gas-filled floats on their fronds. These plants are anchored to the sea floor by a strong holdfast 25 m (80 feet) below.

AUSTRALIAN SEA LIONS

Australian sea lions look as if they have an idyllic life. They seem to spend their days surfing the waves, frolicking in the sea and lounging about on the beach. But in fact these are the hardest-working seals in the world. Australian sea lions live in the marine equivalent of a desert, a place where food is desperately hard to come by. They have evolved a bizarre breeding strategy and phenomenal diving skills in order to survive in these desolate conditions.

The pups need to suckle for an incredible year and a half, the longest suckling period of any sea lion. As a result Australian sea lions can breed only once every 18 months. This non-annual breeding strategy is unique among seals and is the only way they can live in such barren seas. Food is so scarce that hunting dives are also long and deep. The sea lions average about 10 dives an hour, descending up to 100 m (330 feet) each time, and over a third of all the time they spend at sea is on the bottom, where they hunt squid, octopus, fish and crustaceans in the murky depths. These animals are superbly adapted for life underwater and even by seal standards they are extreme divers. In a scientific experiment, one mothering female was observed to have made an astounding 3000 dives during a three-day foraging trip, returning to shore only to feed her pup and rest.

The pups are usually born in sheltered coves adjacent to the main colonies. Just a few days after giving birth the mothers have to leave their offspring to go hunting. Whilst the adults are out at sea the pups are as playful and mischievous as puppies, constantly chasing one another or harassing the local seagulls. But as soon as their mothers return to the breeding colony the youngsters suckle almost constantly until it's time for their mothers to depart on the next hunting trip. At birth the pups weigh about 7 kg (15 pounds) and it takes them a full 18 months to grow to their weaning weight of 35 kg (75 pounds).

At just a few weeks old the pups take to the water for the first time, learning to swim in shallow lagoons before venturing out into the open ocean. Young sea lions quickly acquire the amazing grace, agility and speed of the adults. This is essential not only for catching prey, but also for evading their main predator, the great white shark. Most sea lions can outmanoeuvre sharks, but the slow, weak and unwary fall prey to these efficient hunters. Only about half of all sea-lion pups survive to the end of their second year, because sharks, starvation and storms take their toll, and only a third will reach maturity.

Adults returning from hunting trips surf the waves to shore, saving valuable energy as they speed through the dangerous 'shark zone'. Australian sea lions are fantastic surfers, using their streamlined bodies and extreme diving skills to ride the waves with consummate ease. The swells that hit the south Australian coast create perfect waves and as they surf to shore these sea lions show off their mastery of the underwater world. Silhouetted within the

3

wave face they carve elegant turns and some leap clear from the crests, whilst others catch the foaming breakers right up the beach, where they waddle ashore.

Australian sea lions live at the very upper limit of their physiological capability and have a life expectancy of just 12 years, the shortest of any seal. Today there are only about 12,000 left and they live around the coast from Kangaroo Island in South Australia to the Houtman Abrolhos Islands in the west. Sealers decimated the population in the 19th century and their numbers have still not recovered. Females might not have their first pup until they are six years old and this long period between birth and reproduction is one reason why their numbers are recovering so slowly. So in stark contrast to their laid-back appearance, Australian sea lions face a constant battle to survive.

1. Australian sea lions have an 18-month breeding cycle so pups can be born in winter or summer.

2. They are totally at home underwater and can stay submerged for over eight minutes.

3. Sea lions are very mobile on land, walking along on their fore and hind flippers.

◆ TOPIC LINKS

6.3 Last Refuges
p. 220 Kangaroo Island

THE SOUTHERN OCEAN

The Southern Ocean is the wildest place on the planet. Vicious winds whip up mountainous waves that lash the south coast of Australia, creating the continent's most dramatic coastline. But this violent ocean has introduced some Antarctic richness to Australia's seas. The fertile waters of the Southern Ocean wash Australia's southeastern corner, nourishing shoals of shimmering fish that in turn feed fur seals, dolphins and sea birds. Other Antarctic creatures, such as the majestic albatross, nest here and the fertile waters have even enabled penguins to breed on the shores of this parched continent. Whales gorge themselves in Antarctica for the productive summer months before migrating to Australia's waters to mate and give birth and the few islands that dot this mighty ocean come alive each summer with millions of breeding sea birds and marine mammals. In all these ways, the Southern Ocean pulses life into the seas of Australia.

WILD SEAS

Undisturbed by any significant landmass, huge swells spiral around the frigid continent of Antarctica. Nothing protects Australia from these ferocious seas, so storms batter the length of its southern coast. Relentless weathering of the fragile limestone rock has sculpted awesome cliffs and offshore stacks, none more impressive than the series of towering Twelve Apostles on the coast of Victoria. Thundering waves working over thousands of years have separated these huge chunks of limestone from the mainland, creating the region's most famous natural formations.

In the heart of the notorious 'roaring forties' (▷ p. 33), the waves that beat Tasmania have created a coastline with a rugged beauty, and the south of the island in particular has one of the most dramatic coastlines in the world. Exposed peninsulas jut into the ocean and their steep cliffs are punctuated with dazzling white beaches and eucalypt forests. The confrontation between land and sea creates a dynamic shoreline – water blasts through fissures in cliff faces and gigantic waves beating the shore create loud booms which seem to shake the very land itself. This extraordinarily wet and wild location defies Australia's clichéd image as a flat and arid land.

However, the Southern Ocean brings more than just the erosive power of waves and storms. The easterly flowing Leeuwin Current peters out around Victoria and Tasmania, enabling the cool waters of the Southern Ocean to fertilize these seas and support some of Australia's most productive fisheries. Essential nutrients combine with warm summer days to fuel a rich plankton bloom, which in turn feeds schools of pilchards. These immense silvery shoals attract a whole host of predators. Fur seals, dolphins and

1. Southern Ocean storms can batter the coastline of Tasmania for days on end, producing rugged coastlines such as The Blowhole on the Tasman Peninsula.

The giant Tasmanian crab is one of the biggest crustaceans in the world. One individual weighed a mighty 14 kg (31 pounds) and measured 43 cm (17 inches) across its shell.

gannets corral the pilchards into a tight ball at the surface, where they take turns to feed on the trapped fish. It's a furious sight, with dolphins and fur seals parting the shimmering ball from below while gannets dive into the pilchards from above.

The Southern Ocean has introduced a distinctly Antarctic feel to the coastline of Australia. Fairy, or little, penguins live along the southern edge of Australia and Tasmania. They are the only penguin to breed on the mainland and, at only 50 cm (20 inches), are the smallest of the world's penguins. They hunt small shoaling fish and squid by day, returning to the colony to feed their chicks in the evening. By returning at this time they avoid predatory birds that hunt during the day. As the light fades they approach the coast in tight groups and at dusk come

ashore, cross the beach and head for their burrows behind the dunes. This is the famous 'penguin parade' that thousands of visitors enjoy each year on Phillip Island, Victoria.

Penguins aren't the only Antarctic creatures to nest along the coast of Australia. Every summer 12,000 pairs of shy albatross raise their chicks on a few of the small Tasmanian islands. At this time the adults remain relatively close to the breeding colonies, feeding in nearby waters but, once the chicks have fledged, parents and offspring disperse around the Southern Ocean. These elegant birds soar effortlessly on surface winds and cover great distances to forage for fish and squid. Around southern Australia they are joined in this hunt by other species, such as black-browed and yellow-nosed albatross, which nest on more distant islands.

1. The 2-m (6¹/2-foot) wingspan of these shy albatross is ideal for gliding, but such huge wings can be a hindrance on the precarious cliff faces.

2. (opposite) The towering columns of Cape Raoul, Tasmania, are made of durable granite which is more resistant to the weathering action of the waves.

1

1. Snares crested penguins can walk for 1 km (over ¹/₂ mile) from the shore to their breeding colonies.

2. (opposite) Royal albatross incubate their eggs for 11 weeks, one of the longest incubation periods of any bird.

Overleaf: The towering Twelve Apostles, enormous stacks of limestone, have been separated from the mainland by the erosive forces of the Southern Ocean.

SUBANTARCTIC ISLANDS

The millions of sea birds that feed in the Southern Ocean are forced to visit land to breed, but with only a few islands dotted through this vast ocean huge numbers of birds have to concentrate on these rare, storm-swept locations. Most consist of little more than wind-blown fields of tussock grass exposed to the full fury of the weather, yet every summer they teem with life as dense colonies of penguins, albatross, petrels and shearwaters congregate to rear their young.

Australia's Macquarie Island is one of the world's great penguin strongholds, with 4 million king, royal, rockhopper and gentoo penguins breeding in noisy rookeries. It is close to New Zealand's group of five subantarctic islands – the Snares, Auckland, Campbell, Bounty and Antipodes – which were recently listed as a World Heritage Area. Campbell Island is the world's major breeding ground for the greatest sea bird of them all, the southern royal albatross. This majestic bird has a wingspan of over 3 m (10 feet) and flies an estimated 190,000 km (120,000 miles) each year. The main island of the Snares, just 3.5 km (2 miles) long, has more nesting sea birds than the entire coastline of the British Isles. An estimated 6 million sooty shearwaters breed here, as well as 50,000 endemic Snares crested penguins which nest among the stunted forests.

All the birds that breed on these islands are supremely adapted to life at sea. Albatross, shearwaters and petrels ride the winds with effortless grace and penguins 'fly' underwater with equal beauty. But they all face the challenge of returning to land to reproduce and feed their chicks. The incessant winds that keep the soaring birds aloft make landing on steep cliffs a formidable task, and penguins are often forced to come ashore in furious storms which batter the rugged rock faces. Somehow these robust little birds seem to bounce and scrape their way to land through the huge waves and then waddle to their rookeries to feed the hungry chicks.

These isolated islands also deflect deep water currents to the surface of the sea, creating big up-wellings of nutrients which help feed these multitudes. The concentration of life here is a powerful reminder of the productivity of the Southern Ocean.

GIANT MIGRATIONS

Thousands of humpback and southern right whales spend several months around the shores of Australia, yet the waters simply do not contain enough food to support these giants. So how can so many of these huge whales survive here? Both species spend the summer months feeding in the cold, plankton-rich seas off Antarctica, migrating in winter to the warmer waters of the Australian coast in order to breed. They may travel thousands of kilometres, give birth and suckle a calf all without taking a bite to eat themselves. Their southern feeding grounds are so rich that they can gorge themselves for half the year and build up enough fat reserves so that they don't need to feed for the other half – they almost double in weight during this period.

Humpback and southern right whales feast on krill, tiny shrimp-like animals which proliferate in their billions when months of almost constant daylight combine with the nutrient-rich water of the Southern Ocean. Humpbacks lunge at the dense swarms, taking huge quantities of krill and water into their cavernous mouths. Water cascades out while krill is trapped by the baleen, long bony plates fringed with a fibrous mesh. Sometimes a pair of whales will work together, concentrating their prey by releasing a curtain of bubbles, charging up to the surface through the middle of this bubble net and breaching spectacularly with jaws agape. They squeeze the water out of their mouths by contracting their extended throat pleats and raising their huge muscular tongue, before swallowing a giant mouthful of krill. Feeding like this a humpback can consume as much as a tonne of food a day.

Right whales cruise along with their mouths open, trapping plankton in the fine hairs on their baleen as water passes through. But as the plankton blooms of summer give way to shorter days and cooling seas, the whales turn north towards the warmer but less bountiful waters of Australia.

Both species begin to arrive along the coasts in May and June. Humpbacks migrate right up either side of the continent to Australia's tropical waters, settling in shallow warm water, often in the lee of an island or coral reef. They breed around the Great Barrier Reef and North West Shelf, off Western Australia. Southern right whales usually congregate along the southern coast and are rarely found further north than Sydney or Perth. They often come close to shore, preferring shallow sandy bays near rocky cliffs or headlands, which offer some protection from ocean swells. Soon after the females of both species arrive in Australian waters they give birth, and then suckle their calves on a diet of high-fat milk.

As winter draws to a close and the sun returns to the southern hemisphere, these whales leave the warm waters of Australia and return to the Antarctic to feed, no doubt hungry after their six-month fast.

1. (opposite)
A humpback whale and her week-old calf rest in the warm waters around the Great Barrier Reef. They migrate 2500 km (1550 miles) back to the Antarctic to feed over the summer months.

☆ Male humpback whales have the longest and most complex song of any animal. Their haunting melodies can be heard by other whales over 200 km (125 miles) away.

ISLANDS

ISLANDS OF LIFE

The seas around Australia contain a fabulous diversity of islands. They stretch in a huge arc that curves from the eastern end of Indonesia through New Guinea out into the Pacific and then down south to New Zealand and the subantarctic.

Some of those islands, such as New Zealand and New Caledonia, are very old and home to ancient plants and animals found nowhere else on Earth. Others are still being born, blasted out of the sea today by violent volcanic eruptions. Many are tropical paradises, covered in lush vegetation and inhabited by exotic animals, but some are bleak and windswept, battered by the ferocious storms of the Southern Ocean. No other region on Earth can boast such an incredible variety of thousands of islands of all shapes, sizes and character.

The birth of all of them is in some way associated with Australia – some were indeed once connected to it – but today each is unique, with its own wonderful wildlife, vegetation and landscapes.

Previous page: The steep cliffs of Ball's Pyramid, near Lord Howe island, are a secure breeding site for thousands of sea birds.

NEW GUINEA

Of all the major islands, the closest to Australia itself is New Guinea. It lies barely 100 km (60 miles) beyond Australia's northernmost tip. Until world sea levels rose about 8000 years ago at the end of the last ice age, it was connected to Australia by a large swampy plain. For most of its history it was simply a part of northern Australia, so you might expect it to be quite similar. In fact, it could hardly be more different. While Australia is the flattest continent on Earth, dry, dusty and geologically stable, New Guinea is mountainous, lush, green and forested with dozens of volcanoes and earthquakes that shake the ground almost daily. The character difference is not unlike the energy of youth compared with a tired old parent!

Kangaroos in the trees

If you fly over the island, most of the landscape appears green and forested. Endless jungles tumble from range after range of mountains and then spill out to cloak vast swamps. The tropical rainforests of New Guinea are the third most extensive in the world, after the Congo and the Amazon Basin. They cover about 700,000 sq. km (275,000 square miles) in all, but these are like no others on Earth. In the jungles of Africa, Asia and South America each morning is greeted by a chorus of primate calls – gibbons, colobus or howler monkeys. But here there are no monkeys or apes. Instead, many of the tree-dwelling mammals have evolved from those of Australia, so they are marsupials. In place of monkeys, kangaroos live in the treetops, where they feed on the seemingly inexhaustible supply of leaves and the occasional fruit. They hop from branch to branch in a rather

NEW GUINEA AND NEW BRITAIN

Vogelkop Peninsula
Jayapura
INDONESIA
New
Snow Mts
Mt Jaya 5030 (16,498)
Star Mts
Central Range
Guinea
Southern Highlands
Mt Wilhelm 4509 (14,789)
Sepik
Bismarck Sea
New Ireland
Rabaul
Walindi
Kimbe
New Britain
Lae
PAPUA NEW GUINEA
Fly
Arafura Sea
Solomon Sea
Owen Stanley Range
Port Moresby
Torres Strait
Cape York Peninsula
Coral Sea
AUSTRALIA

Height of land in metres (feet)
3000 (16,400)
2000 (6560)
1000 (3280)
500 (1640)
200 (656)
0

1. Tree kangaroos are the largest tree-dwelling animals in New Guinea and this Matschie's tree kangaroo is one of eight different species.

The largest wild animal in New Guinea is a flightless bird, the cassowary, which stands as tall as an adult human.

ungainly way – not surprising when you consider that kangaroo bodies are better designed for bounding across open plains. But the tree kangaroos have evolved some modifications to help their high-rise lifestyle. Their forearms have grown stouter and more muscular for a stronger grip. Their hind legs have become smaller and some species can move theirs independently of each other, enabling them to shuffle and clamber rather than just hop. Their feet are also broader than those of ground-living roos, with non-slip soles, and they use their long tails for balance. But all this does not add up to a very convincing monkey substitute and they rarely seem truly competent in the trees.

Rainforest leaves may appear to provide an endless succulent feast compared with the dry grasses on which most kangaroos feed, but in fact they are tough, often full of toxic chemicals and difficult to digest. So how do tree kangaroos manage? Their main strategy to cope with this poor diet is to conserve energy – they often remain inactive for up to 90 per cent of the time. When the weather turns cold they even let their own body temperature fall, rather than expending energy keeping warm.

As well as kangaroos, there are many possums in the trees, another echo of the time when Australia and New Guinea were joined. These include eight species of cuscus and none is more colourful than the spotted cuscus. But you would have to be very lucky

1. The New Guinea rainforests are some of the richest on Earth, with about 20,000 species of trees and other flowering plants.

2. There are no monkeys or squirrels here. Instead the forest canopy is populated by agile marsupials like this spotted cuscus.

2

indeed to spot one, even though their coats are frequently patterned with bright orange and white blotches. They are slow, secretive and largely nocturnal. Looking rather like cuddly little bears with long tails, they spend most of their time in the canopy, feeding on leaves, fruit and flowers. They may travel slowly but, unlike the kangaroos, they always appear confident up here. Their hands have a pincer-like grip and their prehensile tail forms an additional grasping limb, so they can hang on tight. To increase the friction

further when it curls round a branch, the final two-thirds of the tail is naked, with rough bumps on the inner surface. Remarkably, this is very similar in design to the tail of a howler monkey.

The forest floor is also home to a variety of marsupials. The spotted cuscus has a relative, the ground cuscus, that burrows under-ground. It hides during the day in shallow tunnels beneath tree roots or even in caves, emerging at night to feed on fruits and small animals such as insects, rats and lizards.

Down here on the ground there are also several species of dainty little forest kangaroo. Their small size and slim build enable them to move through the thick forest vegetation with ease in search of succulent shoots and leaves.

Although they have relatives in Australia, most of New Guinea's marsupials are unique. They have evolved to survive in the specific environmental conditions of this island, which include not only vast rainforests but also massive mountain ranges.

THE WORLD'S MOST BEAUTIFUL BIRDS

When the preserved skins of New Guinea's birds were first brought to Europe in the 16th century, people could hardly believe their eyes. Never before had such richly coloured and exquisitely fashioned feathers been seen. These early specimens had no feet or legs and there seemed an obvious explanation – such extravagant birds must come from the heavens, where there was never any need to land. Hence they were called birds of paradise. Later it was discovered that the collectors had merely cut off the limbs to tidy them up, but the name stuck. It could not be more appropriate.

1

Of the 43 kinds of bird of paradise, 38 inhabit the forests of New Guinea, including the most colourful ones. In most species males and females look very different. The females are generally dull, often with brown backs and a barred front. As mothers they need to be camouflaged and inconspicuous when sitting on the nest, but the males are fabulously adorned. The male superb bird of paradise carries a two-pronged, iridescent blue shield on his breast; the emperor supports a bushy fountain of the finest white feathers imaginable; the king of Saxony sprouts a bizarre pair of feathers from behind his ears that are twice as long as his body, each supporting 40 or more blue enamel discs; the aptly named magnificent boasts a golden back, a metallic green breast, twin tail feathers that curl in circles and a mouth that positively glows when opened; the ribbon-tailed simply has the longest tail of any bird in the world relative to its size. The superlatives go on and on and are not restricted to appearance. These birds also perform the most stunning and complex courtship displays.

None is more spectacular than the Raggiana bird of paradise. It performs most vigorously in the early morning, just as the first rays of the sun hit the jungle canopy. A number of males gather high in a single tree, in which they have cleared an arena by stripping away many of the leaves. Each has his own perch and as the sun rises they assume their position and plump out the gorgeous golden-red feathers that sprout from their flanks. Suddenly there's a cacophony of noise and activity. A female has arrived. The males throw out their brilliant plumes, shaking them in extravagant fashion, clapping their wings over their backs and calling vigorously. The dull brown female hops from perch to perch, inspecting this ostentatious activity. The males desperately try to outdo each other. She will mate with only one of them. As the males hang upside down to impress her even further, their plumes cascade from their bodies like golden fountains, catching the early morning sun. Suddenly she is beside one and he explodes in a frenzy of activity, even striking at her. In a moment he is on top of

her and in a matter of seconds mating is all over. This must be one of the most spectacular displays of any animal on Earth, but why these particular birds and why in New Guinea?

Male birds can indulge in this sort of extravagance only if they can be sure the female can bring up the chicks alone, without their help – a male tied to the nest would have no use for bright plumage to attract another mate. This usually means the female has to be able to find sufficient food. Birds of paradise eat mainly fruit and their stout beaks and strong feet are capable of breaking open the toughest and most nutritious types. In forests elsewhere in the world squirrels or monkeys would take these fruit, but here there is no such competition. A rich and readily available supply of food allows the males literally to leave the females holding the babies. Another factor is the absence of mammalian predators such as cats, dogs or foxes, which means there is less danger in growing conspicuous and unwieldy plumage. As a result a whole range of the most beautifully adorned male birds has evolved.

2

But there are exceptions. High in the mountains, in subalpine forest up to 4000 m (13,000 feet), lives one of the most curious birds of paradise of all, the Macgregor's. Males and females are virtually identical, mostly black but with yellow wing patches and large yellow wattles around their eyes. Unlike most birds of paradise they are monogamous and males spend most of their time with their partner. At this altitude there is not much to eat and the Macgregor's specializes on the fruit of just one tree, the southern pine. When they are not fruiting in abundance it almost certainly takes the efforts of both parents to raise the chicks in this bleak alpine world. So the male is not free to indulge in the flamboy-ant promiscuity of other species, but has to be a good father. He remains dull but dutiful.

3

1. The male Wilson's bird of paradise flashes like an exquisitely patterned jewel in the dim world of the forest floor.

2. The flamboyant display of a male Raggiana bird of paradise is designed to impress females.

3. Huli men decorate their elaborate wigs with the feathers of several different kinds of birds, including birds of paradise.

◆ TOPIC LINKS

5.1 Islands of Life
p. 160 Misty mountains

Misty mountains

New Guinea is among the most mountainous islands on Earth. Like a spine down its centre, the ranges run for nearly 2000 km (1250 miles) and rise to a staggering 4884 m (16,000 feet). These are the tallest mountains between the Himalayas and the Andes. The highest peak of all, Mount Jaya, supports glaciers just a few hundred kilometres from the equator. These mountains are also amongst the fastest rising on Earth. The Huon Ranges on the northeast coast have grown to over 4000 m (13,000 feet) in less than 100,000 years, which is a phenomenal rate by world standards, and they are still rising. The reason for all this mountain-building is that Australia is slowly drifting northwards, crashing into the sea floor of the Pacific Ocean. The New Guinea mountains are buckling up along that collision line, like the crumple zone of a car in a head-on smash.

These mountains have brought about much of the great diversity of life on New Guinea. Their sheer height creates a variety of habitats, from lowland swamps and jungle up through various types of mountain forest to alpine meadows, tundra, rock and even ice. Each habitat is home to its own range of animals and plants. The numerous ridges and valleys also break up the landscape and isolate the wildlife on different peaks, so that new species have evolved in each of the various mountain ranges. One striking example is a bird of paradise, the astrapia. On five separate mountain ranges there are five different species: the Arfak, Huon, splendid, Princess Stephanie's and ribbon-tailed astrapias. The latter, from the central highlands, is truly spectacular, with the male trailing a white tail five times longer than its body.

In their isolation, some mountain birds have evolved the most extraordinary behaviour. The Vogelkop bowerbird is cut off on a remote peninsula in the northwest. In one mountain range the males build low, woven towers covered by stick huts so massive that a child could crawl inside. In front there is a lawn of bright green moss. The garden and floor of the hut are decorated with colourful pieces of fruit, bark, flowers, fungi and insect wings. This structure is spectacular enough, but on a nearby mountain the same species has developed an even more sophisticated style. It incorporates several tall maypoles decorated with pandanus leaves eight times bigger than the bird. The decorations on the ground tend to be all of one type, whether it be snail shells, stones, acorns or beetle cuticle. Each individual seems to have a personal preference. The bird even paints some of these objects with a glossy white substance from its droppings. This is quite simply the most elaborately decorated structure built

BIG BUGS

In the jungles of New Guinea many of the insects are spectacular and strange, but some are also giants. These forests are home to the world's largest moth, the Hercules moth, about the size of a small dinner plate. Giant millipedes and weevils (right) roam the forest floor. Spiky stick insects, larger than mice, hang inconspicuously below branches. And there's even a fly that has a head wider than any other. Its eyes stick out sideways on stalks up to 55 mm (nearly 2 inches) long – that is three times greater than its entire body length. Not surprisingly, it's called the stalk-eyed fly. Only males have these extraordinary appendages, so it is assumed that they have some sexual importance. But perhaps the most beautiful of the island's record holders is the Queen Alexandra's birdwing. It flies through the canopy with a wingspan of almost 30 cm (12 inches), making it the world's largest butterfly. Only the females grow to such a size and the difference is clearly apparent in their courtship dance. The male pursues a female, flying closely behind her, seeming to mimic her every move in an exquisitely beautiful aerial ballet until finally mating takes place.

1. (opposite) Rainfall in the mountains can be as high as 10 m (33 feet) a year, creating numerous streams and waterfalls.

by any animal anywhere in the world, and all to impress a mate.

Mountain mammals may not be so showy, but they are often just as strange. None more so than the long-beaked echidna – or giant spiny anteater, as it is sometimes called. This is a mammal that lays eggs, like its Australian relatives the duck-billed platypus (▷ p. 42–3) and short-beaked echidna. It uses the extraordinarily long beak after which it is named to probe the ground for giant earthworms and other invertebrate prey. It then hooks them with a unique barbed tongue. Echidnas are spiky, like giant hedgehogs, but these mountains are cold, so for insulation the long-beaked echidna grows thick fur, which almost hides the long spines beneath.

Other mountain animals develop similar protection. The silky cuscus is a relative of the spotted cuscus, but has much thicker, shiny fur. When really cold it simply curls up into a furry ball. The pygmy ringtail possum uses a different strategy to keep warm, collecting

moss that drapes the trees and building a cosy nest with it. Surprisingly there is even a snake up here, Boelen's python. So how does a cold-blooded animal like this survive? Its scales are a velvety black, perfect for absorbing the limited heat from the sun in these cloudy mountain conditions. On bright days it slithers out onto a mossy bank or rock to bask in the warm sunlight.

The highland forests are magical worlds of twisted trees, with trunks and branches smothered in colourful fungi, ferns, moss and lichen. Mist often hangs late into the day, turning the trees into spooky silhouettes. At higher altitudes the forest gives way to open tree-fern savannahs, alpine tussock, grassland, even tundra, with tiny alpine flowers such as dwarf rhododendrons and bright blue gentians creating a splash of colour in this damp and often overcast world.

The weather up here is extremely wet. Tall mountains rising out of a warm, tropical sea create torrential rainfall, in some places up to 10 m (33 feet) a year. Bogs are extensive and

numerous small streams run off the slopes. Tumbling over rapids and waterfalls, spilling down the mountain ramparts, eventually they coalesce into large rivers that thunder towards the coast.

Water worlds

In the centre of New Guinea sit the Star Mountains and from here two of the largest rivers on the island start life, just a few kilometres from each other. The Fly plunges south towards the Gulf of Papua, travelling 1200 km (800 miles) to the sea, making it the longest of the island's rivers. In terms of the volume of water it discharges, about 13,000 cubic metres (over 450,000 cubic feet) every second, it is one of the most powerful rivers in the world, ending in a vast delta system of shifting islands and shallow channels, with a mouth over 80 km (50 miles) wide. To the north the Sepik tumbles into a vast floodplain, a network of twisting channels, hidden lakes, extensive swamps and numerous floating islands.

1

2

The Sepik is the most fascinating river system in New Guinea. For a start its huge floodplain is surprisingly new, built just 6000 years ago when sediment washed down from the mountains filled up a large inlet of the sea. The main river is fed by numerous tributaries that wind through vast networks of lakes and swamps, creating a complex maze of waterways. Floating vegetation covers large areas of water, making progress impossible by either foot or boat. In places, isolated lakes blossom with thousands of waterlilies, the mud at their edge ablaze with the large pink blooms of lotus. Lily-trotters strut across the floating lily pads and white pygmy geese glide by in elegant pairs. But remarkably, very few native fish swim here. The young age of the river system has simply not given them time to colonize in any numbers. Today carp and tilapia have been introduced, but before that a few tarpon, gudgeon and catfish were all the locals had to catch. On the other hand, such a large river allows marine fish that can tolerate fresh water to migrate upstream from time to time, including sawfish and sharks. Large saltwater crocodiles also inhabit most of the waterways, penetrating up to 1000 km (625 miles) inland. This is not the place for a casual swim!

Despite the swampy conditions, lack of fish and dangerous crocodiles, people do live here. But it's not easy. Malaria is rife, travel difficult and the swamps do not support normal crops. Instead the staple is sago, a native palm from which the pith is extracted to make pancakes or a kind of sticky porridge. In spite of these difficulties, the Sepik region supports some of the greatest variety of human culture on the whole island. Large and impressively decorated spirit houses and fabulous carvings adorn many villages. New Guinea is full of such paradoxes. In terms of wildlife, people, climate and landscape it is by far the most diverse island in all of Australasia, a magical place full of surprises.

FRUIT BATS

Throughout Australasia the most widely distributed mammals are bats because they can fly from island to island. The strongest travellers of all are the large fruit bats. With powerful wings, some think nothing of flying 50 km (30 miles) a night in search of food. They keep their weight to a minimum by having hollow bones, as birds do, and their gut can digest a meal in under half an hour, so they don't need to fly with a full stomach.

New Guinea can claim to be the fruit-bat capital of the world, with almost 50 different species, and they are not difficult to see, especially the big flying foxes which roost in large camps. The most famous is in the coastal resort of Madang, where groups of casuarina trees in the town centre provide homes for several thousand spectacled flying foxes. The sight, sound and smell of so many bats are almost overwhelming. Even during the day they barely seem to sleep and the camp is alive with their moving bodies and constant calling, but the most impressive spectacle is at dusk. Thousands upon thousands of dark silhouettes take to the air against the deep red of the setting sun, wave upon wave passing overhead, reminiscent of squadrons of wartime bombers. Their flight is slow and deliberate and they head off in all directions in search of food, but before they feed some of the bats engage in a more unusual activity. Flying low over Madang lagoon they dip into the sea. Are they simply drinking water or taking in salt? Nobody really knows.

The hills of New Guinea are full of caves, potential homes for bats. But, unlike their

1. A tube-nosed fruit bat hanging from a fig leaf on the island of New Britain.

2. Bare-backed fruit bats leave their shelter, a large limestone sinkhole in the rainforest.

1

smaller cousins the insect-eaters, most fruit bats cannot echolocate, so they are not able to navigate in the pitch blackness of a cave interior. The single exception is the Rousettus fruit bat, which uses a simple system of clicks to echolocate. However, members of another group, the bare-backed fruit bats, use the parts of caves where light penetrates. Again there is a wonderful example of this near Madang – a huge limestone sinkhole in the middle of the rainforest, its overhanging walls providing shelter for hundreds of thousands of bats. It is quite a feat for such large animals to descend into such a hole, but the wings of this species are designed for manoeuvrability. They spiral out of the sky in tight circles, tipping their wings from side to side to spill air, twisting, turning and diving to avoid others in their way. The wall in front is smothered in bat bodies; there is rarely any vacant space. But each incoming flier selects a spot and heads straight for it. At the last moment it spreads its wings to brake, turns upside down and grasps the rock. The neighbours move aside a little and a living ripple spreads across the wall as thousands of nearby bats adjust their position. It's an extraordinary sight.

New Guinea has the most species of fruit bats, but New Britain probably has a greater concentration in a small area. It has 14 species, the smallest just 15 g ($^1/_2$ ounce), the largest 100 times that weight. The tiny blossom bats concentrate on flowers, feeding on nectar and pollen with their absorbent, mop-like tongues. Tube-noses, on the other hand, are fig specialists. They are some of the most extraordinary-looking bats of all, with brightly spotted fur and long, snorkel-like nostrils. Their distinct colour patterns provide camouflage: during their day they hang beneath vegetation, where their yellow spots break up their outline in the dappled sunlight. Their snorkels allow them to breathe with their faces stuck inside a juicy fig. New

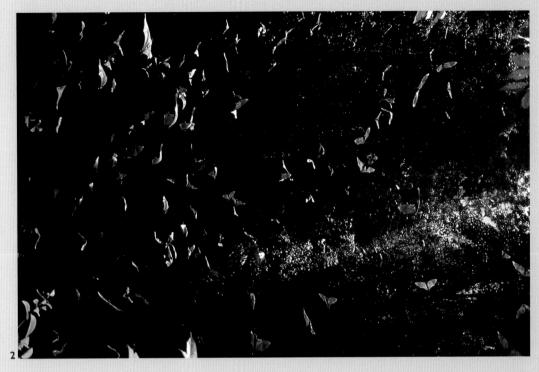

2

Britain also has bare-backed fruit bats and various flying foxes, including the largest of all, the greater flying fox, weighing over 1.5 kg (3$^1/_2$ pounds) and with a wingspan of 1.5 m (5 feet). But most fascinating of all is the masked flying fox. It is easy to recognize with its bizarre white face divided in four by a black cross. Nobody knows the purpose of these distinct markings, but could they again be camouflage? Like the tube-noses this bat roosts under vegetation, hanging in pairs. Unusually, the male secretes milk. Could this be a mammal in which fathers breast-feed their young? It seems possible but, like much about the bats here, it has never been observed and so the details remain a mystery.

As you travel further east and south, away from New Guinea, the number of fruit bats reduces as the ocean crossings involve greater distances. Only one species has managed to reach the large but remote island of New Caledonia. Even on islands where they were once common, fruit bats are declining because

clearance for logging, agriculture and plantations is removing their habitat and the larger ones are often eaten by people. These wonderful animals are essential for dispersing the seeds and pollinating the flowers of numerous native plants, so their disappearance endangers the future of the very forests they live in.

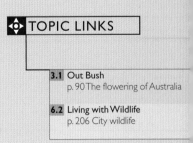

◈ TOPIC LINKS

PACIFIC JEWELS

Stretching in a broad band east of New Guinea and then south lie chains of thousands of islands, dotted like emeralds through the Pacific. The birth of all of them was in some way connected to the geological activity around the edge of the Australian continental plate. Because of this many are volcanically active, like New Britain, New Ireland, the Solomons and Vanuatu. Others are older volcanoes whose fires have now died, such as Lord Howe Island. Most have risen directly out of the sea and never had a connection with any other land, so their wildlife arrived by either sea or air. Their isolation makes each island fascinatingly different. Perhaps most unusual and distinct of all is New Caledonia, which started life as a chunk of eastern Australia and broke away during the days of the dinosaurs. Whatever the origin of these islands, their remoteness, unique wildlife and scenic splendour make them some of the most intriguing and beautiful places on Earth.

Previous page:
The seas around
New Guinea contain
hundreds of small
islands built on the
top of coral reefs.

NEW BRITAIN

Lying just off the northeast coast of New Guinea, New Britain is a large mountainous island, over 500 km (300 miles) long. About halfway along its northern shore, the Williamez Peninsula juts out into the sea, creating a bay called Kimbe. This location typifies the violent but life-promoting nature of this exotic island. The peninsula itself is built from a series of dramatic cone-shaped volcanoes rising directly from the sea. Geysers, hot springs, bubbling rivers and sulphurous fumaroles erupt out of the jungle-clad shore. In the sea the tops of now-extinct volcanoes rise close to the surface, creating a fabulous series of coral-encrusted sea mounts, teeming with colourful life.

New Britain is on the Pacific 'Ring of Fire' and one of the most geologically active places on Earth. Some of the animals here take advantage of that. Just a few kilometres inland from Kimbe Bay the tangled forest encloses a series of steaming pools and rivers, where hot volcanic water gushes to the surface. This geothermal activity also warms the surrounding soil to the perfect temperature for one bird, the megapode, to incubate its eggs.

Megapode means 'big foot' and this bird uses its large feet as trenching tools to excavate beneath the forest floor. Tunnelling a metre or so (over 3 feet) into the soft soil, the megapode finds a depth at which the temperature is just right for incubation, before laying a clutch of eggs. Covering them with more

soil, the mother then leaves them, having nothing further to do with either eggs or chicks. In the soil the eggs risk being dug out by monitor lizards or collected by local people, who regard them as a valuable delicacy. If they survive these dangers the chicks hatch after six to nine weeks and then face their greatest challenge: they have to tunnel their way towards the light. It's a long struggle, taking several hours. Many chicks don't make it, but those that do appear above ground as fully formed miniatures, ready to fend for themselves. A yolky egg full of nutrition, and incubation in the warm volcanic soil, have given them the start they need. Judging by the tens of thousands of megapode holes that litter every corner of

1. Tuvurvur volcano, near the town of Rabaul on New Britain, has been continually active since its last massive explosion in 1994.

forest around the hot springs, it's a successful strategy.

In the middle of the bay, volcanic activity creates other opportunities for life. Dormant volcanic peaks below the surface provide wonderful platforms for coral growth. With many of these small reefs dotted across it, and sheltered from winds and waves by the Williamez Peninsula, the peculiar geography of Kimbe Bay helps support one of the richest coral-reef communities anywhere. Over 400 species of coral grow in this one bay, as many as on the entire length of the Great Barrier Reef. And the variety of colourful corals is not the only attraction. On a short dive on a typical reef not much larger than a tennis court you might also see a shark or two; packs of jacks attacking large schools of bait fish; hawksbill turtles; razor fish or a pygmy seahorse hiding in bright red sea whips; giant Napoleon wrasse; exquisite mandarin fish; glass shrimps; huge barrel sponges; moray eels; several types of anemone fish … the list is almost endless. You can dive the same spot a dozen times and still find new animals and witness fresh behaviour.

Kimbe Bay is special, but there are many other fabulous bays on this island and many, many more tropical islands in the sea around New Britain. This part of the world is also relatively unknown – a fabulous region for biological explorers and adventurous visitors alike.

1. (opposite) Feather stars festoon a huge barrel sponge in Kimbe Bay, on the island of New Britain.

VOLCANO TOWN

Many of the islands of Australasia are highly volcanic, but if you had to identify the most dangerous location of all, the town of Rabaul on New Britain would be hard to beat. It was almost completely wiped out twice during the 20th century. Rabaul lies on the edge of a beautiful bay surrounded by hills. The bay is a caldera, a giant collapsed volcano over 5 km (3 miles) wide, and many of the hills are active volcanoes, vents for the enormous heat and pressure below. One of those is Vulcan. On 28 May 1937 the residents of Rabaul felt earth tremors and then the sea floor rose, lifting a cargo ship clean out of the water. The following morning Vulcan exploded, sending a column of ash and pumice 10 km (6 miles) into the sky. Thunder and lightning crashed all around and the falling debris killed about 500 people. The town was rebuilt but then destroyed again in 1994, when Vulcan and Tuvurvur, a volcano on the opposite side of the bay, exploded simultaneously. Vulcan erupted for hours, but all these years later Tuvurvur still steams poisonous gas and spews the occasional rock. Fortunately the town was prepared and few people lost their lives. Since then a new town has been built 30 km (20 miles) away, safer but certainly not out of reach of the power of the volcanoes.

LORD HOWE – SEA BIRD CITY

Picture in your mind the perfect Pacific island – green and lush with long, palm-fringed beaches, a beautiful coral reef and lagoon, rolling hills, stunning sea cliffs and, at one end, towering mountains draped in beautiful rainforest. And imagine if all this were blessed with a near perfect climate, often described as perpetual spring. This is Lord Howe, one of the most idyllic islands in the whole Pacific.

When New Zealand broke away from Australia 80 million years ago it created a ridge of weakness in the ocean floor. Over time many volcanoes broke through. Lord Howe is one of those, and it first rose from the seabed between 6 and 7 million years ago as a large volcano, about 30 km (20 miles) across. Since then it has become extinct and now almost 98

per cent has been worn away by the wind, rain and sea to create the small but beautifully formed island of today. But visit and enjoy it while you can – in just another 200,000 years it will be washed away completely!

Being a small island, over 500 km (300 miles) from the Australian coast and with no other land nearby, Lord Howe is biologically very isolated. Only animals that could fly, raft on the sea or be blown by wind have found a home here. So the only mammal is a single species of bat, the only terrestrial reptiles two types of lizard. When people first discovered the island in 1788 Lord Howe supported 15 species of land bird, of which 13 were found nowhere else on earth. Sadly a combination of hunting and the accidental introduction of rats in 1918 has driven nine of these to extinction. Today just the wood hen, currawong, golden whistler and white-eye

remain, along with the sacred kingfisher and emerald ground dove, which are also found in Australia.

However, the most spectacular of all Lord Howe's birds are not those that live on land but the sea birds that use the island and surrounding islets to breed. A small speck in a vast expanse of ocean, this is the only place to nest for hundreds of kilometres around. So each year huge numbers of sea birds of 14 different species descend on Lord Howe. Most arrive in spring, and none in greater numbers than the sooty terns. Some of these agile fliers nest on the main island, but the largest colony is on tiny Roach Island, just offshore. Like all the small islands that surround the main one, it's difficult to land on and has steep, rough slopes. So Roach has not been settled and rats have never invaded, allowing sea birds to nest undisturbed on the ground.

1. Sooty terns are the most numerous of Lord Howe's breeding sea birds.

2. Lord Howe Island has the most southerly coral reef in the world, the result of warm currents flowing down from the Great Barrier Reef.

Overleaf: Sooty terns hover over Roach Island, with Lord Howe's cloud-capped mountains in the background.

2

Sooty terns are the sports cars of this sea-bird world – elegantly styled in neat black and white trim, with astonishing speed and aerial agility. Fully loaded with fish for their young chicks, they rush towards the ground, spilling wind from their wings, using their feet as delicate air brakes and pulling up into a hover. So light are they that at this point the strong winds blowing in off the Pacific Ocean often blast them backwards before they get a chance to touch down. Watching hundreds of terns attempting this together on Roach Island in a stiff breeze, with the towering mountains of Lord Howe in the background, must be one of the world's most inspiring wild scenes. Undaunted, the little birds always try again and again until finally, with a nifty tuck of their wings, they are on the ground – to be assaulted almost immediately

by hungry chicks. In the confusion you'd think they might feed anyone, but they recognize their own youngster by voice and deliver a fishy meal into the correct mouth.

The other great sea-bird sight on Lord Howe is the tropic birds. They court on the wing, especially along the spectacular sea cliffs that line the southeast coast. The males display by flying in a series of backward loops. As one starts others join in. Steadily the group climbs, each male trying to outdo the others with his aerial ability. Standing on the lip of the cliffs you can often see hundreds of these gleaming white birds synchronously spiralling below, against the backdrop of a brilliant turquoise sea. This is one of the largest breeding colonies of red-tailed tropic birds in the world, and few can have such a stunning setting.

⭐ Near Lord Howe Island, Ball's Pyramid is the world's tallest sea stack. This spectacular spire rises 551 m (1807 feet) from the ocean and is home for a great variety of sea birds.

NEW CALEDONIA – A GLIMPSE INTO THE PAST

Approached from the sea, New Caledonia appears to be similar to many other Pacific Islands – lush and green, surrounded by a coral reef and lagoon. In fact the reef surrounding the main island of Grand Terre is huge, second in size only to the Great Barrier Reef. But closer inspection of the vegetation suggests this is a unique place. Strange pines and monkey puzzles dot the shore and hill-sides. This is not a typical oceanic island, but a remnant chunk of continent that sliced off the east coast of Australia some 80 million years ago. Since that time it has been isolated with its cargo of ancient plants. It now supports two-thirds of the world's monkey-puzzle trees, as well as many other unique conifers.

At the time it broke away flowering plants had only just appeared on Earth and today, of New Caledonia's 3000 or so species, 80 per cent are found nowhere else.

This unique flora grows on unusual soils. Over time, New Caledonia has been subjected to the geological equivalent of a turbulent washing machine, with the result that its rocks are all jumbled up. Indeed, many rocks from the deep sea floor now lie on land. These heavy rocks contain a cocktail of metals such as manganese, chromium, nickel and magnesium heaved up from the depths of the ocean. Many of the unusual plants here are now adapted to grow in these 'contaminated' conditions which would poison most other vegetation.

Isolation since the age of the dinosaurs means there are no native mammals here, except a fruit bat. But there are lots of lizards. In fact for its size New Caledonia contains far more species of lizard than anywhere else in the Pacific and possibly in the world. Over 80 per cent are unique. The lizards are of two kinds, skinks and geckos, including six species of giant gecko, one of which is the world's largest. At over 30 cm (12 inches) long, it's the size of a rat. Rather curiously, it has webbed feet, although it lives in the forest canopy. Here it uses tree holes as safe places to rest and lay its eggs. If threatened, it inflates its body with air to appear even bigger and hisses loudly. If that is not sufficient deterrent, it also has a strong bite. Although the dinosaurs have long gone, the absence of mammals and the sheer numbers of unique lizards make this one of the few places where you could say that reptiles still rule.

1. Like almost all species of New Caledonian lizards, this giant gecko is found nowhere else on earth.

2. The unique kagu, displaying in New Caledonia's rainforest.

3. The landscape and flora of New Caledonia give it a distinct feel, very different from any other islands in the Pacific.

⭐ New Caledonia was given its name by Captain Cook in 1774 because the mountainous terrain reminded him of the Scottish Highlands.

New Zealand is one of the strangest places on Earth. Few other locations have such a weird assortment of animals and plants living in such spectacular and varied scenery. What other group of islands can boast parrots that live in snow, bats that tunnel underground, giant grasshoppers bigger than mice and flightless birds that behave like hedgehogs? These animals inhabit a world of mystical ancient forests, fiery volcanoes and explosive geysers, towering snow-capped peaks and deep ocean fjords.

Since the land that would one day make up New Zealand broke away from Australia it has remained isolated from the rest of the world. No other island so large has remained so cut off for so long, its animals and plants free to evolve in their own unique way. New Zealand is such a remote place that it was also one of the very last locations on the planet to be discovered and settled by people.

THE CREATION OF NEW ZEALAND

Maori legend tells how South Island was originally a canoe belonging to Maui, the sky father, and Papatuanaka, the Earth mother. They anchored their canoe to a rock which today is called Stewart Island and then fished North Island up out of the sea. This may sound a fantastical tale, but the real story is just as fascinating.

About 80 million years ago, a portion of the Earth's crust broke away from the east coast of Australia to form a very long 'New Zealand', stretching across several thousand kilometres of Pacific Ocean. Later it shrank to a string of small, low-lying islands almost submerged by the sea. Then it drifted from the tropics to colder, temperate waters. Huge geological forces built powerful volcanoes and pushed up massive mountains. Glaciers carved them into spectacular peaks and then, at the end of the last ice age just 10,000 years ago, the ocean flooded vast areas of the coast.

1. A winter landscape, beside Lake Tekapo on South Island.

NEW ZEALAND

Hauraki Gulf
Auckland
White I.
North Island
Tasman Sea
Rotorua
L. Taupo
Mt Taranaki 2517 (8255)
Mt Tongariro 1968 (6455)
Mt Ruapehu 2797 (9174)
Cook Strait
Wellington
South Island
Kaikoura
Southern Alps
Mt Cook 3733 (12,244)
Christchurch
PACIFIC OCEAN
Milford Sound
Queenstown
Fjordland
Dunedin
Foveaux Strait
Stewart Island

Height of land in metres (feet)
2000 (6560)
1000 (3280)
500 (1640)
200 (656)
0

That extraordinary history has created the spectacular New Zealand you see today – and the landscape is still changing.

The islands of New Zealand lie at a point where several of the Earth's continental plates meet. Under North Island the Pacific Ocean floor is sliding under the edge of the Australian continental plate and the heat generated has created a string of active volcanoes – Tongariro, Ruapehu, Ngauruhoe and Taranaki (formerly Egmont). The most active volcano of all is White Island, just off the northeast coast, which erupts more or less continuously. On the mainland nearby is the town of Rotorua, known as 'Sulphur City'

because of the foul sulphurous smell that always hangs in the air. In amongst the buildings, plumes of steam rise from the numerous hot springs, bubbling mud pools and geysers, which erupt regularly with explosive force. It is a fascinating thermal wonderland.

On South Island the continental plates push past each other rather than slide over and under. The enormous pressures created by this grating do not build volcanoes or geysers, but they have rucked up the spectacular Southern Alps. These extend like a snowy spine for almost the entire length of the island.

1. The boiling mud pools of Whakarewarewa, on the edge of Rotorua town.

2. The New Zealand alps stretch like a spine down much of the length of South Island.

Overleaf: The bright colours at the edge of Champagne pool, at Wai-O-Tapa, are created by mineral deposits.

 FJORDLAND

The New Zealand mountains rise almost straight from the ocean, creating a stunning coastline of snow-clad peaks and tumbling glaciers. Some of the glacier-carved valleys are flooded by the sea, creating spectacular fjords. The most famous is Milford Sound (left). From the snow-capped top of Mitre Peak, almost 1700 m (5500 feet) above, the world's tallest sea cliff drops almost vertically into the deep waters of the sound. Here the underwater ecology is unique. Heavy rainfall cascading down the granite slopes picks up tannins from decaying vegetation and takes on the colour of tea. It is less dense than sea water and in the calm conditions of the sound floats as a layer on top, cutting down the penetration of light. Black and red corals, which usually live deeper than 40 m (130 feet), now grow in profusion in the dimly lit shallows, creating beautiful marine gardens.

PARROTS IN THE SNOW

The Southern Alps of New Zealand, like the mountains of New Guinea, are some of the newest and fastest rising in the world. They have been created largely in the last 5 million years, a blink of the eye in geological time, and are still rising at about 17 mm (2/3 inch) a year. The tallest is Mount Cook, at 3733 m (12,244 feet).

Lying in the path of the 'roaring forties' (▷ p. 33), the mountains receive a great deal of rain that falls as snow all year round on the higher peaks. This has built large permanent glaciers. Over thousands of years these have carved the peaks into spectacular spires and ridges. Because the mountains are relatively new in geological time they rise steeply, and the glaciers slide down them at great speed. The Franz Josef glacier, which tumbles precipitously towards the sea, has been recorded as moving an astonishing 7 m (23 feet) a day.

The Alps are home to many animals that elsewhere in the world do not live in such high mountains. These include lizards, cicadas, grasshoppers, wetas and, perhaps most fascinating of all, parrots. The kea is the world's only alpine parrot and in winter lives well above the snow line. At first sight it seems just a large, dull green bird, but watch one for more than a few minutes and the real kea emerges. As it flies, feathers hidden under the wings flash a brilliant red, making this one of New Zealand's more colourful birds, and its personality is even brighter than its plumage.

These birds live a relatively long time – up to 20 years or more in the wild – so have an extended childhood. That allows them time to learn the tricks they need to survive in this harsh environment. They are highly social

1

2

and gangs of youngsters fly around the snow-fields exploring almost every object in sight. At first they just look, often from every angle, but then use their powerful beaks to pull things apart. In the wild this involves mainly rocks, vegetation and anything edible. It is an important part of their education. But there are now ski resorts in these mountains, with much more interesting items to explore. The gangs of young parrots descend on cars, pulling apart the rubber trim, bending aerials and biting ski racks. They seem to be involved in a detailed and very physical investigation of their environment. It is fascinating to watch – unless you own the car in question, of course! They also raid the ski-field restaurants for discarded food to supplement their diet. In the wild their taste is very broad, ranging from plants to insects, grubs, worms and the eggs of other birds. In the Kaikoura Mountains groups of keas have also been seen pulling shearwater chicks out of their burrows and eating them. On occasion they have even attacked sheep. They are an incredibly versatile parrot with considerable intelligence, often compared favourably with primates, which is how they received their nickname of 'mountain monkeys'.

★ Hairy grasshoppers living in the snowfields of New Zealand have an extraordinary escape mechanism. They ski, using their rear legs as poles and their ribbed belly as the ski.

3

1. Franz Josef glacier tumbles down from the Southern Alps.

2. In winter keas live well above the snow line, the only parrot in the world to do so.

3. Keas use their beaks to investigate everything around them, including the rubber trim on cars at ski resorts.

MAGICAL FORESTS, STRANGE CREATURES

Because of New Zealand's long isolation, over three-quarters of its plants are unique, giving the vegetation a very special character. Before the Maori arrived, about 1000 years ago, perhaps 85 per cent of the land was forested. Three main groups of trees, the kauri, podocarps and southern beeches, are representatives of the ancient forests of Gondwana. They all have seeds that cannot float on water, so their ancestors must have been here when New Zealand first split away from Australia. Both kauri and podocarps are conifers and the southern beech also hangs on to its leaves all year round, so much of New Zealand's forest is evergreen, almost as colourful in winter as in summer.

Like the plants, most of the animals here live nowhere else on Earth. With no land mammals to compete with, birds have come to dominate the forests. When early European explorers arrived there were birds everywhere and they described the dawn chorus as almost deafening. Sadly, since that time, almost half the native birds have become extinct. Introduced mammalian predators such as cats and stoats are largely responsible for this dramatic decline. Never having seen such hunters before, the birds simply did not know how to respond when stalked and attacked. Many are flightless, too, which makes them even more vulnerable. Despite this tragedy New Zealand still retains a fascinating variety of unique birds: the agile kokako which runs along branches like a squirrel rather than fly far; the energetic saddleback which chases after insects both in the canopy and on the forest floor; the tui, the male and female of which both have a melodious song; six species of unique parrots; and many more. However, none typifies New Zealand more than the flightless kiwi.

1

1. High rainfall along the western coast of South Island creates numerous waterfalls, such as Mackay Falls on the Milford Track.

2. The tui, one of New Zealand's unique birds, is an excellent mimic, able to imitate the calls of other birds and even cats and people.

2

 KAKAPO – THE DISAPPEARING PARROT

The kakapo (left) is a very odd bird, the world's largest parrot. At over 3.5 kg (nearly 8 pounds), it is flightless, nocturnal and nests underground. But it's really famous because of its record as the slowest breeding bird of all. A mother may raise a chick successfully only once every decade or two. By the middle of the 20th century the kakapo was one of the most endangered birds on Earth, on the brink of extinction. Desperate action was required. Males were located in remote Fjordland valleys, but no females could be found. For decades conservationists searched the wildest parts of South Island without success. But eventually, in 1977, a handful of females was located on Stewart Island. The entire population was relocated to a few predator-free islands and brought under intensive care. Today every nest is monitored remotely by miniature spy cameras, chicks are weighed every few days, mothers given food supplements and if necessary their youngsters are hand-reared until they can fend for themselves. It is a massive and expensive operation, but is beginning to work. From a few birds in the early 1980s there are now almost 100. Maybe the world's slowest-breeding bird has a future after all?

The six species of kiwi are like nothing else on Earth. Their closest living relatives are ostriches, rheas, emus and cassowaries. Within New Zealand, their closest relatives were the moas, giant flightless birds which were hunted to extinction by the Maori several hundred years ago. In many ways kiwis are more like mammals than birds. They are nocturnal and use a strong sense of smell to locate earthworms, insects and other invertebrate prey in much the same way as a hedgehog or badger would. They sprout hair-like plumage and long whiskers like a cat's. Their bones do not contain the typical air cavities of most birds, but are filled with marrow, like a mammal's. Curiously, the females also have two working ovaries, the same as many mammals but unlike a typical bird. Even their body temperature is mammalian rather than avian. Why should this be? Because there are no ground-living mammals like hedgehogs or badgers to compete with, kiwis have simply been able to exploit these vacant niches. With that change in behaviour over time came gradual evolution of a body form which better equipped them for this particular way of life.

If kiwis are the bird equivalent of hedgehogs, then giant wetas are the insect equivalent of mice. Wetas are rather like large, grotesque-looking grasshoppers and some forms have barely changed in the 200 million years this group has existed. In New Zealand there are five different types: cave weta, tree weta, tusked weta, ground weta and giant weta. The biggest, at 45 g (1^{1}/$_{2}$ ounces), is larger than a mouse. They emerge at night and scurry over the forest floor in search of a wide variety of plant and animal food in much the same way as mice do. They were able to do this presumably because there were neither mice to compete with nor nocturnal mammalian predators to hunt them. Today, unfortunately, both have been introduced and so giant wetas survive only on a few offshore islands which rodents and predators have not reached.

Although there were no original ground-living mammals, two species of bat fly through New Zealand's forests – the long- and short-tailed bats. Short-tails are particularly fascinating as they have begun to adopt a ground-living existence. Although they are fast and agile fliers, they spend a considerable part of the night crawling around on the forest floor, hunting for invertebrates such as worms and wetas. They even tunnel under leaf litter in pursuit of prey. Again, it is the absence of mammalian competitors or predators on the forest floor that has enabled this unique behaviour to develop. In time might these bats even have evolved to become completely flightless, like many of the birds? Sadly, because of the introduced carnivores that now patrol forest floors throughout New Zealand, we will probably never know.

★ Relative to their own size, female kiwis lay a larger egg than any other bird. It can be nearly 20 per cent of their body weight.

1

1. The largest of all the kiwis, the great spotted kiwi can weigh up to 4 kg (nearly 9 pounds) and stand almost 50 cm (20 inches) tall.

2. The tuatara is the last remaining member of an ancient group of reptiles that evolved at the same time as the dinosaurs.

ISLAND REFUGES

With the spread of introduced predators, many of New Zealand's unique creatures are now extinct or dramatically reduced in numbers on the two main islands. But there are over 600 smaller islands, from the subtropical Kermadecs in the north to the subantarctic Snares and Auckland Islands in the south. Many are virtually predator-free and retain their original vegetation, making them ideal refuges for endangered species. They have literally saved many species from extinction. The striking black and red North Island saddleback, a bird that feeds on the forest floor, was wiped out from the mainland by the end of the 19th century. But a handful survived on Hen Island in the Hauraki Gulf, off the coast north of Auckland. From these few individuals the numbers have now grown and populations are established on a number of other small islands. Nearby, on the forest-covered Little Barrier Island, the stitchbird similarly survived extinction, and this one location now sustains more endangered bird species than any other in New Zealand.

Perhaps the most unusual island survivor is the tuatara. It looks rather like a small dragon and you would think it was a type of lizard. But it's actually the sole relic of an ancient group of reptiles called the sphenodontids, which first evolved on Earth 220 million years ago. It originally lived on the mainland but disappeared soon after Europeans arrived, surviving only on offshore islands. Stephens Island, which lies in Cook Strait, between North and South Islands, is the most important, with about half the total population of 100,000. The tuatara lives life in the slow lane, which is probably why it was so vulnerable. Apart from being a sluggish mover, it takes time over breeding. After a female mates she keeps the eggs inside her for about nine months, then lays them in the soil, where they will lie for a further year or more before hatching – the longest incubation period of any reptile. It will then take the hatchlings 10 years or so to achieve sexual maturity, another 15 to 20 to reach full size and they may live for a century. There is one more curious aspect of tuatara life – they inhabit the burrows of ground-nesting sea birds such as shearwaters and petrels. The burrow provides a safe shelter and the bird droppings attract insect prey. What does the tuatara do in return for such hospitality? It often eats the eggs or young chicks of its host!

There is perhaps no better example of the weird and other-worldly nature of New Zealand wildlife, a whole ecology that has grown so strange as it evolved in isolation for a long period of time.

NEW WORLDS

HUMAN FOOTSTEPS

For more than 60,000 years people have learned how to live in Australia's huge landscape. During that time, the continent has seen great changes, both natural and man-made. Some animals have proliferated while others have disappeared for ever, and each human culture has left its mark.

The first people to set foot here probably came from Southeast Asia, and they rapidly spread across the continent, adapting over millennia to survive in deserts and forests, mountains and coasts. By contrast, Europeans came to Australia only recently. In 1770 Captain Cook saw it as an ownerless land and claimed it as a British territory. The first colonists wanted to make a land that looked like home, and the changes they made were profound.

In some places the landscape and its wildlife have been altered beyond recognition, but Australian nature can also be tough and it has responded with some surprises.

Previous page: The Opera House and Sydney Harbour Bridge today. It was here that the first British settlers made their mark on the land.

LAND OF THE DREAMING

In the wide sandstone country of Australia's far north the heat of the day is intense. Tiny lizards dart away to shelter and kites wheel overhead in a sky so blue it is almost metallic. The landscape feels remote and barely touched, but high on shadowy rock faces there are paintings. Some are of people, but many are of animals: turtles and wallabies, geese and fish; some life-sized, many drawn with incredible detail. Some are painted as 'X-rays', showing the internal organs of the animals. The earliest of these paintings may be 23,000 years old, possibly the world's oldest. Whoever made those rock paintings of ochre and charcoal would have had an intimate knowledge of the land, the seasons and the animals, vital for survival in this volatile place.

Aboriginal Australians lived throughout the mainland and islands for 3000 generations, in hundreds of different tribal groups. They inhabited the rich woodlands of the south, the bitterly cold mountains and the burning centre. They hunted kangaroos, lizards and emus and gathered plants and insects, according to the season. At rivers and coasts they caught fish, shellfish and turtles; in the desert they were guided to water by watching finches and parrots.

For this way of life, techniques had to be learned and wisdom passed on. Aborigines explained their relationship with the natural world through stories, known as the Dreaming. It answered questions about how the land was created, and where humans and animals came from; it told of spirit ancestors who took forms such as kangaroos and snakes and then became the trees and rocks, and even the rain and the sunlight. People and

1. Aboriginal rock art, such as this example at Kakadu, shows an intimate relationship with the natural world. People have lived in this area for at least 25,000 years and possibly much longer.

The first European to report seeing a kangaroo was an officer on Captain Cook's ship. He sketched it – then ate it.

nature were one; as much a part of eternity as the animals and plants, the rivers and the stars. Many natural landmarks had, and still have, particularly deep spiritual significance. The huge red monolith of Uluru (▷ p.68) is regarded as a landscape created by ancestral beings, still present in the sacred rocks.

The Dreaming stories arose from the daily, close observation of the natural world, and wove in cautionary tales suggested by the animals' appearance and behaviour. There are symbolic stories of spirit animals and how they lived. In a society with no written language, it was a way of passing on the skills needed for survival, and it laid down laws as to how the land and all its inhabitants should be regarded. Some animals were 'taboo' for

some or all of the time as a way of protecting them from being over-hunted. 'Story places' were areas where spirits lived and humans were forbidden to enter, but within them animals could thrive, safeguarded for the future.

The earliest people to come to Australia would have encountered a very different set of animals, including huge beasts which are now extinct. There was a giant wombat and a carnivorous kangaroo, an enormous duck-like bird and a marsupial lion. Fearsome as they sound, these animals seem to have died out suddenly about 30,000 years ago and it has been suggested that Aboriginal hunting pressure helped their extinction. Evidence is sketchy but it's clear that Aborigines did alter the landscape; most dramatically, they set it

1. 'Firestick farming' was practised by Aboriginal people for thousands of years. It cleared vegetation and made hunting easier, but it required skill.

2. Early European settlers recorded the way Aboriginal people hunted animals and gathered plants for food, but remarked that they didn't settle or cultivate the land in a way familiar to European eyes.

1

on fire (▷ p. 108). Fire was a tool that cleared the land and allowed clear views for hunting; animals would run from the blaze and be easy to bring down. As vegetation was burned off in patches, fresh growth would return, attracting grazing kangaroos, which could also be hunted.

Thousands of years of deliberate burning may have changed the vegetation of Australia, favouring those plants that were best adapted to survive. This 'firestick farming' was practised with considerable skill. Desert grasses like spinifex burn phenomenally quickly and fires can race off over vast areas, so burning had to be done at the right time, leaving refuges for some wildlife to escape. Without this carefully developed fire regime, wildfires would rage like infernos, taking everything with them.

The balance between humans and nature has always been a delicate one in Australia and Aborigines developed an intimate relationship with the difficult land on which they ultimately relied for sustenance. However, today many of the links with the land are being broken and traditional lifestyles survive only in fragments. Arnhem Land, in the far north, is a mysterious place of tropical forests, rivers and rocky gorges and no non-Aboriginal may enter without permission. Here, in one of their last cultural strongholds, the country's traditional owners live in the old way, hunting geese and kangaroos, and gathering shellfish and yams, maintaining the land as they would have done long before Europeans came.

When Europeans arrived they colonized Australia swiftly and the Aborigines were removed from the land. After all those generations of Aboriginal occupation, the newcomers would change the face of this continent country in just 10. The effects of their earliest endeavours live on today.

2

1. Sydney in 1845, less than 60 years after the first British settlers arrived. Early painters often portrayed the landscape to look more 'English' than it was.

2. Many native animals must have seemed half-familiar to European eyes. Black swans are native only to Australia.

3. Curious-looking echidnas bear a passing resemblance to hedgehogs – but they lay eggs.

FROM ENGLAND TO AUSTRALIA

On a warm spring evening in November, in a suburb of Melbourne, a song very familiar to British ears floats in the air. Amid the traffic noise and streetlights, a blackbird is singing, sweet and powerful, its voice carrying across the rooftops. It's as attractive here as it is in an English garden, but blackbirds don't belong in Australia. In fact there are lots of animals in Australia that shouldn't be here.

In 1770 Captain James Cook landed in Botany Bay, near what is now Sydney, and claimed the land for the Crown. Eighteen years later, a British colony was founded, chiefly as a convenient place to send convicts. Those early arrivals, and the free settlers that followed, found a land full of novelties. It was all rather unsettling: the seasons were the wrong way round, with snow in August and baking heat in January. Even landscapes and plants that at first looked vaguely familiar turned out to be completely strange. As for the animals, they were baffling and, to some eyes, rather a disappointment. There were no large four-legged animals, no cattle, no deer; instead there were kangaroos that were impossible to round up. There were no melodious songbirds; instead there were colourful but raucous parrots. Something had to be done.

These were days when it was regarded as a noble thing to 'improve' on nature, with a special emphasis on 'useful' animals. Australia was a country 'half supplied with the requirements of civilization', as one writer remarked and so the new colonists set about changing things. Sheep and cattle, brought in by the first ships, were soon doing well; by 1860 there were 4 million cows and 20 million sheep being raised. But there was still room for more improvement and in the mid-1800s 'Acclimatization Societies' were busy bringing in what they regarded as useful and ornamental wildlife from all over the world.

All sorts of animals were tried. Llamas and alpacas were imported and released. Queen Victoria sent red deer as a gift to Queensland. Scientists wanted to turn the seemingly empty interior, regarded as a waste of land, into a kind of Africa by releasing giraffes, antelope and yaks, suitable for hunting and transport, but without the dangerous additions of lions or gorillas. Some thoughtful men even wanted to release monkeys to make the eucalypt woodlands around Melbourne a bit more interesting and give travellers something amusing to look at as they rested under the gum trees on a hot day. The Governor of Victoria stated that he didn't like monkeys, but he thought it would be a good idea to release boa constrictors to eat up the venomous snakes that were so troublesome. Fortunately,

none of these crazier ideas came to fruition.

Other animals were brought in just to give settlers, missing the country they'd left behind, a memory of home, and some of these introductions did succeed. Blackbirds and nightingales were brought from England and released in Melbourne. While the nightingales failed to thrive, blackbirds did and are now regarded as a serious pest across the country, damaging fruit and competing with native birds. They are a prohibited species in Western Australia and are destroyed if they are found there.

Much of the activity of Acclimatization Societies sprang from ignorance of Australia's ecology, and their objective of 'stocking our waste waters, woods and plains with choice animals' was certainly misguided. Many of the animals that were brought in did not survive for long because they found themselves in conditions that did not suit them, but those that did would have a serious impact on Australia's animals and plants.

3

2

Baron von Mueller, the government botanist in Victoria in the late 1800s, was very fond of blackberries and scattered seeds through the wilderness to feed poor travellers. It is now Victoria's worst introduced weed.

Animal vagabonds

Living alongside Australia's native wildlife there's a whole range of foreign animals that are now causing such havoc that they are putting the natives in peril. The most successful were those that were tough and adaptable enough to cope with the vagaries of the Australian landscape and climate, and they increased their numbers spectacularly.

Early British colonials, keen for something to shoot, brought rabbits from home. Twenty-four rabbits were released into southern Victoria in 1859, and shooters and fur trappers made great efforts to assist their spread across the country, which would turn out to be the fastest of any colonizing mammal anywhere. Famous for their breeding abilities, adapted to a harsh environment and without native predators to stop them, rabbits in their millions invaded virtually the entire country, devastating crops and outcompeting native burrowing mammals for habitat and food. Rabbit-proof fences failed to stop them and introduced

diseases have held back their numbers only temporarily, so new control techniques have to be continually developed, even now.

A whole ark's worth of animals has been brought to Australia and settled in. Pigs, escapees from the very first colonists' ships, have turned wild and roam in groups of up to 60 through the wetter parts of the continent, trampling waterholes and digging up the eggs of reptiles and ground-nesting birds. In the tropical wetlands of northern Queensland there's the incongruous spectacle of crowds of wild pigs wandering among wallabies and huge black-necked storks. Goats are another destructive invader, successful because they can eat virtually anything, so they thrive on Australia's nutrient-poor vegetation.

Some animals have become part of Australian culture. Wild horses, called brumbies, are celebrated in poetry, evocative of the mountainous landscape of the southeast. Here, the descendants of horses that wandered from early colonists' farms live tough lives, agile and fast in the

snowbound highlands. Others have settled on the grassy plains of the interior, their grazing causing problems when numbers get too high.

But perhaps the worst invader to find itself at home in Australia is the fox. Homesick English gentlemen, missing the hunt, brought in European foxes in the 1860s and chased them with English hounds. But the foxes, superb generalists, spread like wildfire across much of the country, from desert to suburbs. Next to dingoes, they're the biggest predator on the mainland. They can eat fruit and berries, insects and carrion, but their preferred prey is live animals. They have been blamed for the extinction of many populations of small native mammals; numbats and small wallabies, perhaps too naïve to recognize such recently introduced predators, are among those decimated.

In areas where foxes have been removed, these marsupials have begun to recover. As much as anything, this is a tribute to the resilience of the native wildlife in the face of so much human meddling.

☆ There have been Australian animals on the loose in Britain. A number of red-necked wallabies escaped from an English zoo in the 1940s and until recently lived wild in the Peak District.

1. The European red fox, introduced by English gentlemen in the 1860s so they could hunt in the style of the Old Country. Now foxes are serious predators of native wildlife.

2. (opposite) Wild horses, known locally as brumbies, are descended from early settlers' stock, and have become part of Australian culture.

1

CANE TOADS

This is the story of how a simple error of judgement introduced a pest that now seriously threatens major parts of the Australian ecosystem.

The tropical northwest of Queensland, with its warmth and rain, is well suited for growing sugar cane and by the 1930s this crop was being cultivated in large areas, although it is not native to Australia. However, a local beetle had taken a fancy to it and was chewing its leaves and roots so voraciously that the canes were collapsing and dying in hectares. Something had to be done to save the new sugar industry.

The same problem was being encountered in other parts of the world where sugar cane was grown as an exotic crop, and it seemed a solution was at hand. Some large, beetle-eating toads, collected from their natural homes in the rainforests of South and Central America, had been introduced to the cane-fields of Hawaii and appeared to be doing the trick. The toads were eating the offending beetles and their grubs with relish. In 1935 desperate Queensland farmers sent a man to Hawaii to collect some of these heroic toads so that they could be released into the Australian canefields.

A hundred or so toads were packed up and taken to Queensland, a journey that took three weeks. To the delight of the farmers, they survived the journey well and even started mating. It seemed as if the plan was going to work. The toads were released among the cane and anxious farmers watched and waited.

But there was a problem. In Hawaii, beetles had lived low down in the cane and the toads were able to catch them, but the Australian

beetles moved much higher above the ground and were simply out of the toads' reach. In addition, the cane fields were too dry for these big amphibians to thrive and they soon took off in search of more comfortable surroundings.

In the 70 years since they were introduced, cane toads have spread into a fifth of the continent, west into the Northern Territory and almost as far south as Sydney. They move fast, in some areas advancing at up to 27 km (17 miles) a year. And these toads are big; they can grow to weigh almost 2 kg (4½ pounds) and up to 15 cm (6 inches) long. But why are they such a problem? Well, to begin with, they reproduce at an alarming rate and, for another thing, they're seriously poisonous.

As long as there is water available, cane toads will breed, whether it's in a natural waterway or a suburban garden pond. They can even tolerate slightly salty water, hence their scientific name, *Bufo marinus*, the marine toad. A female can lay more than 20,000

eggs, far outnumbering any native frog. The young grow quickly, hatching into tadpoles in three days and in just three weeks they are ready for a life on land. As adults they have voracious appetites, largely for insects, but they may also eat small snakes, lizards and mice, which they take into their large mouths whole. Intriguingly, they've also developed a taste for dog food, which they will steal from a bowl under the very nose of the dog.

But it is the toads' toxicity that is the real problem. Glands on their shoulders exude a powerful poison, a cocktail of 14 chemicals that act on the heart and nervous system, causing convulsions, hallucinations and death to virtually anything that tries to eat it. Some birds have learned to avoid the dangerous parts of a cane toad's body, but the toads have poisoned dogs, snakes and goannas, and even crocodiles have been found dead with cane toads in their mouths.

The big worry is that they are beginning to poison native animals. Northern quolls, which live in the tropical woodlands of northern Australia, are carnivores and will happily tackle a toad. But any quoll unfortunate enough to eat one would be doomed. Numbers of quolls, which are already low, have declined in areas where cane toads are known to be. Now it seems that the toads have infiltrated Kakadu National Park, the jewel in Australia's natural history crown and full of unique wildlife (▷ p. 110). Some scientists are concerned that native frogs and other larger animals will suffer as a result of the presence of this enormous, poisonous amphibian, but at present there's little that can be done to stop its advance.

Drive through the suburbs of Queensland on a wet night and the chances are you will come across a cane toad creeping across the road, large and squat and warty. They are not welcome in Queensland any more, but it's hard not to feel a little sorry for these adaptable animals; it wasn't their choice to come to Australia, and the error was all human.

1. Sugarcane fields in northern Queensland. Cane toads failed to clear the pest beetles, and these insects are still a problem nowadays.

2. A cane beetle – the pest that led to the arrival of a bigger pest.

3. Toxic toad: Cane toads have glands on their shoulders that exude powerful chemicals.

◈ TOPIC LINKS

6.1 Human Footsteps
p. 198 Animal vagabonds

LIVING WITH WILDLIFE

In the 200 years that Europeans have lived in Australia, rapid changes have been made. Pioneer farmers have opened up the outback, finding a living in the often difficult landscapes of Australia's vast interior. Cities have grown quickly, most hugging the more comfortable environment of the coasts, and these are where the vast majority of people live. Cities are home to over 80 per cent of Australia's population, which is the most urbanized in the world.

Everywhere people have settled they have come into contact with native wildlife. While some animals have declined as a result of the human changes, others have adjusted to life alongside their human neighbours. People, too, have had to learn to live with the creatures they have found around them. From urban kangaroos and house-raiding possums to deadly spiders in the garden, the relationships between people and animals in Australia are incredibly varied.

AT HOME ON THE RANGE

On an outback farm in South Australia, in the dust of a late summer morning, there's a spectacular sight. Thousands of little corellas, small white parrots, cluster on fences and windmills around the farmstead, noisy and squabbling, some of them swinging about upside down for fun. They have come here for a free feed: the contents of a full grain bunker and the spilt seed that is scattered around. They descend on the bunker in an immense white cloud and, undeterred by the tarpaulin that covers the grain, they rip into it with their beaks until they make a hole big enough to get their head inside. Then they eat their fill. The farmers try to discourage them by firing shots, but they're not that easily scared: they just fly round and land again. Natural seed-eaters, these little corellas are taking full advantage of human efforts to make a living from the landscape.

Over the last two centuries, hardy pioneers have pushed into the outback and established remote farms. The first settlers thought that cultivation would be easy and that even the desert could be made to bloom, using the farming techniques brought from the Old Country. But Australia is a tough and unpredictable place, with extremely infertile soils and erratic weather. In bad drought years crops withered and sheep died, and the relics of abandoned farmsteads mark the places where many farmers failed in this sunburnt land.

What was needed was water. Sheep and cattle can graze the sparse salt bush and native grasses of the interior, but they must

1. Cattle being mustered in Queensland. Raising stock in Australia's outback has always been reliant on finding sources of water in the huge rangelands with their unpredictable rainfall.

have access to reliable water supplies. Therefore thousands of bores were sunk, tapping Australia's vast natural underground reservoir, the Great Artesian Basin (▷ p. 74), to fill artificial waterholes. Now, no sheep or cow is much more than about 5 km (3 miles) from water, even in the long dry months.

Domestic animals weren't the only ones to benefit. Native animals, too, need water, and the artificial water sources were a boon to them. Seed-eating birds need to drink daily and the water inadvertently provided by farmers has meant they can thrive even in the most arid regions. Budgerigars, which wander inland areas, gather in their thousands to drink at these waterholes, and zebra finches visit cattle troughs in huge noisy flocks. Emus also stride in to drink, their numbers possibly increasing due to these reliable water sources.

Kangaroos, which would naturally be restricted by the limited amount of water available for most of the year, visit these man-made waterholes in great numbers, and they too are thriving. There may be 25 million red kangaroos alone, more than there are people in Australia and possibly more than the fragile grasslands can support.

In times of severe drought, native wildlife relies even more heavily on sustenance from farms and can cause serious damage. In Western Australia in the long dry summer of 1932 farmers asked for the army's help to stop the advance of thousands of hungry emus which they feared would decimate their crops. The soldiers went after them with machine guns, but the birds, which can run at 50 km (30 miles) an hour, were too quick for them and the 'Emu War' was called off.

Farming in the outback takes a certain resilience of character. The nearest town might be five hours' drive along the red dust of an unsealed road, and drought or deluge are equally likely but equally unpredictable. For the vast majority of Australians living in sophisticated towns and cities, the association with nature may seem to be less intense but, even in urban areas, wildlife has managed to make its home alongside people, and some animals are thriving.

SEARCHING FOR THE NIGHT PARROT

In a land of beautiful birds, why has a smallish, dumpy green parrot become one of the most sought-after in Australia? The night parrot (right) looks like a fat budgie with big feet. It seems to be mostly nocturnal, a poor flier and it spends most of its time in grassy undergrowth in the arid lands of the centre. But other than that little is known about it. It was never very common and it seems that changes in burning patterns, and the spread of introduced predators, may have reduced its numbers even more. Few had been seen since the 1880s and it was assumed to be extinct, seen only as long-dead specimens in museums.

But then, in 1990, a squashed one was found by the side of a road. Searches were mounted and publicity campaigns begun. Long-distance lorry drivers were asked to keep their eyes out for this cryptic little bird. In 1996, at a remote cattle station beyond Alice Springs, the station owner and a scientist working on camels spotted one drinking at trough. There have been no reliable sightings since. Does the night parrot still exist? While tantalizing evidence appears, the search continues and this little green bird has become something of an Australian legend.

1. (opposite) Many of Australia's birds are nomadic, flying long distances in search of food and water. Seed eaters like corellas have thrived alongside farms where grain and water is more easily available.

1. Campers in the bush relax alongside western grey kangaroos in Western Australia. Kangaroos vastly outnumber people in Australia, and some thrive around human settlements.

2. Common brush-tail possums are found in most places where trees grow, even in urban areas. They'll eat a wide variety of leaves and fruit, taking household scraps when they're available.

3. For a flightless bird like an emu, walking across the road may be an unavoidable hazard.

CITY WILDLIFE

There's no mistaking a brush-tail possum living in your roof. Active at night, they tread heavily and noisily as they prepare to go out in search of food; if disturbed they'll growl and screech. Common brush-tail possums, with their soft grey fur, big ears and bushy tails, are probably the native mammals most people are familiar with because they are highly adapted to city life. Although their natural homes are in tree hollows in forests, they will quite happily take up residence in the shelter of houses, in spaces above ceilings or under floors. Their normal tucker is leaves and fruit, but they will also raid dustbins and are particularly partial to roses.

Possums thrive in towns because they are so adaptable. When cities grow quickly the animals that do best are those that can cope with the changes and even take advantage of humans. In modern urban Australia there are plenty of native animals that live cheek-by-jowl with people. Free food is always a great attraction. Have a summer barbie and you might find a kookaburra swooping down and stealing the sausage from your plate. Flying foxes visit urban street trees at night to feed on their fruit and blossoms.

Golf courses, with their well-watered grass and patches of trees, are a great attraction to wildlife, including kangaroos. In a dry country like this, if there's fresh green food and plenty of water around, it's a desirable kangaroo habitat and they can thrive in high numbers. Normally shy animals, they sit quite relaxed in the sun while people putt around them. Some of them live their whole lives on the greens,

munching grass and raising their young, exactly as they would in the bush.

Many animals find themselves in cities simply because the buildings have grown up around them and taken over their natural habitat. Brush turkeys – large, ground-dwelling birds of the northern rainforest – live on insects and seeds that they find by scratching around the leaf litter with their big feet. They also build large mounds of soil in which to incubate their eggs. However, rain-forests have largely disappeared and, where homes have been built on them, brush turkeys will make do by living in people's gardens, especially if they have been planted with rainforest plants. In the leafy suburbs of Brisbane brush turkeys carry on their usual habits of kicking the soil around and building their nest mounds, with no regard for

Sulphur-crested cockatoos, attracted to people's homes by the offer of food, sometimes create havoc by chewing wooden window frames, even causing the window to fall out.

carefully tended borders and delicate garden plants. If a mound is destroyed the male bird will simply build another one. Fortunately, many householders have learned to tolerate these hefty birds, as their natural habitat is under continuing threat.

Anywhere in Australia the wild is never far away and all sorts of unexpected animals live alongside people. The green tree frog occurs all through the east and north, where it likes cool, damp places. In drier areas, it is often found near human habitats – particularly in outside toilets, which are perfect providers of the humidity it needs. It might be disconcerting to find a green tree frog beaming at you from the toilet bowl, but they are quite harmless. However, there are other Australian animals that, should you happen to meet them, are rather more alarming.

DANGEROUS AUSTRALIANS

Australia has the world's most venomous spider. It also has more venomous snakes than any other country, and the most venomous known lives here. In its waterways swim the world's biggest and most lethal reptiles. Humans here have always had to live alongside some very dangerous animals.

The first European settlers had to contend with a range of hazards. Pioneers clearing 'the scrub', the steamy rainforest of the northern coast, wrote of cruel heat and lashing rain, fever and exhaustion. Crocodiles infested the rivers and venomous snakes, creeping about their homes and outbuildings, had to be contended with. The further people pushed into the outback, the more dangers they faced.

Snakes have long struck fear into people,

and Australia has more than 100 species, of which 25 can cause people harm, although most are shy and avoid humans wherever possible. The inland taipan is the world's most venomous land snake, with toxin 50 times that of the Indian cobra, but it lives in the remote floodplains of inland Queensland, so the chances of meeting one are low. But as farms spread so did rodents, and some snakes came looking for them. The snake that has killed most people recently is the eastern brown snake, which often visits farmlands and barns in search of rats and mice, even reaching the suburbs of Adelaide and Sydney. Just a minor bite from this snake can cause rapid death.

Saltwater crocodiles, too, can come uncomfortably close to people. Although they're found only in the tropical north, that includes the city of Darwin, which is built beside prime crocodile territory. These extremely dangerous animals, some nearly

2.5 m (8 feet) long, are taken out of Darwin Harbour on a regular basis. Well over 100 a year are caught in traps and removed to crocodile farms, but there's no guarantee that the harbour is crocodile-free. As crocs can leap out of the water with no warning and run faster than people, it pays to be cautious around northern waterways.

For the most part dangerous animals are encountered less frequently in cities than in remote areas, but there are some dramatic exceptions. When one of the most deadly goes by the name of the Sydney funnel-web it is clearly a town-dweller. The Sydney funnel-web is a serious spider, 6 cm (2 inches) long, with a shiny black body and enormous fangs strong enough to penetrate a fingernail. It loves damp gardens and may actually have increased in numbers as houses have spread. It lives in burrows, with triplines of silk trailing out to catch unwary prey. Its venom can kill a

★ The Australian inland taipan, the world's most venomous snake, carries enough toxin in its venom glands to kill over 12,000 guinea pigs.

1

person in less than two hours and so it's considered to be the world's most deadly spider.

Males roam around on autumn nights looking for females and they often fall into swimming pools or wander into houses, climbing into shoes and linen. If disturbed, they lift their body up, grip their victim and plunge their fangs downward. Fourteen people are known to have died since 1927 due to being bitten by the Sydney funnel-web. For some mysterious reason, primates, including humans, are sensitive to their venom, while other animals such as rabbits are barely affected. Fortunately, anti-venom is now available and today deaths are very rare.

Wildlife here can certainly be hazardous, but to put things into perspective, recent statistics show that in a 10-year period, while one person died of a spider bite and 11 of shark attacks, over 30,000 died in road accidents. Humans are by far the most dangerous Australians!

2

1. The eastern brown snake has extremely potent venom and strikes very rapidly if threatened. Introduced rats and mice around farmland are a favourite prey.

2. The Sydney funnel-web, which may be the world's most deadly spider, is found around human habitation.

 PIED PERIL

One of the most surprising urban dangers comes from the sky. Australian magpies are capable of putting people into hospital. These melodious black and white birds, no relation of European magpies, are familiar around town. But in spring, when the nesting season begins, things can turn nasty. Australian magpies are highly territorial and when they nest in urban areas, as they often do, they regard humans as potential predators. So in preparation for the time when their defenceless young leave the nest, they set about clearing the area with an aerial bombardment.

Pedestrians and cyclists are targeted as these large birds swoop and dive to attack with great precision. People have even had their eyes pecked. Children seem to be particularly at risk. It's not only the parent birds that attack – magpies form large social groups and non-breeding adults join in the defence of the nest.

Passers-by are warned to avoid nesting areas if at all possible. Other advice is to carry an umbrella, or to wear a sturdy hat with eyes drawn on the back of it, as the feeling of being watched seems to make magpies less likely to attack.

6.3   LAST REFUGES

This island continent has been separated from the rest of the world for over 40 million years and so it is full of animals and plants that have evolved in isolation and are found nowhere else on Earth. That means that if any of these unique species are lost, they are lost for ever. In fact Australian species are becoming extinct at an alarming rate. Exquisite marsupials and beautiful birds that were common two centuries ago are disappearing. In the last 200 years Australia has lost 19 mammals to extinction, more than anywhere else in the world. Dozens more may be sliding towards oblivion. Scientists believe one in five bird species may vanish and four extraordinary frogs are feared lost for ever. Why, in this huge and sparsely populated land, should this be, and is there any hope for the animals that are hanging on by a thread?

The answers are sometimes surprising because, in Australia, things are not always what they seem.

GOING, GOING, GONE

On 7 September 1936 the world's last thylacine died at Hobart Zoo in Tasmania. Some 50 years later it was officially declared extinct. Its loss is especially poignant because there are photographs and film footage of it padding round its cage, and people still alive who can remember it in the wild.

The thylacine was a stripy, dog-sized, carnivorous marsupial that once lived throughout Australia, hunting kangaroos and wallabies. But when dingoes were introduced by Asian seafarers, about 4000 years ago, the thylacine was outcompeted and vanished from the mainland. It found a refuge in Tasmania, where there were no dingoes, but its small population was pushed to extinction by hunters early in the 20th century. It was finally given protection under Tasmanian law in 1936, much too late to save it.

The thylacine is one of dozens of native Australian animals lost for ever and many were charismatic and beautiful. The paradise parrot, an exquisite, long-tailed bird that nested in termite mounds, was once common in arid regions, but it is almost certainly extinct – no-one has seen it since 1927. Many species are now known only from pictures, like the toolache, an elegant wallaby which was hunted for its fur and had all but vanished by the 1920s.

To lose any species is sad, but many of Australia's vanished species were extraordinary. The pig-footed bandicoot, a small mammal with orange-brown fur and long ears, had curious front feet with just two functional toes and claws that looked like pigs' trotters. It has been extinct for at least 50 years.

What has happened to Australia's animals? Many have suffered from the changes that European settlers made to the countryside as vast areas of bushland were cleared for farming, and domestic animals ate the

1

2

1. The mala, a little wallaby once widespread in the centre, has been seriously threatened by introduced predators, and it is in danger of extinction. Great efforts are being made to save it.

2. The end of the line: the last known thylacine, or Tasmanian tiger, died in captivity in 1936.

grasses that sustained much of the native fauna. As Aborigines were moved from their traditional lands, their techniques of burning the vegetation, practised over thousands of years (▷ p. 108), came to a halt. The unmanaged landscape could burn out of control and many small animals could not survive. Introduced predators, such as foxes, also threatened native mammals.

In the face of these onslaughts some of the remaining animals are barely surviving and great efforts are now being made to save them. The northern hairy-nosed wombat is one of the most endangered animals in Australia. Named for the fine hairs on its nose, this stocky little marsupial has been reduced to just 70 animals in one tiny area of central Queensland. Its numbers probably fell because it had to compete with cows

for grazing, especially during severe droughts. The remaining population is being very carefully monitored and cattle have been excluded from its territory. But the northern hairy-nosed wombat is still in serious trouble.

In some cases more drastic remedies are tried. The mala, a dainty little wallaby, was once widespread through Australia's western deserts, but it too fell foul of European changes: competition for food with sheep and cattle, changes in traditional burning practices and, worst of all, introduced predators. By the 1950s only two tiny wild colonies remained, and these were brought into captivity to save the species. They bred successfully and careful efforts were made to reintroduce them to the wild. But every animal released disappeared, eaten by foxes and feral cats.

Something else had to be tried if mala were not to become extinct. One solution was to put them somewhere no predators could reach: on an island. The one chosen was desolate Trimouille, off the coast of Western Australia. It had been used as a testing site for nuclear weapons by the British in the 1950s, but levels of radiation had dropped by the 1990s to a point considered safe for both people and mala, and the habitat suited them. So these little wallabies were shipped there and they are now thriving among the nuclear artefacts.

For medium-sized mammals, introduced predators, especially foxes, seem to be a key factor in their demise. Places on the mainland that are predator-free are rare, but there are still many island locations where natives can thrive, even if at first glance some appear less than wildlife-friendly.

DINGOES

On a rock face in northern Australia there is an ancient painting of a thylacine, a carnivorous marsupial that was once widespread but disappeared from the mainland 2000 years ago. Almost certainly its demise was caused partly by the dingo.

Although dingoes are often thought of as 'natives', they were brought into Australia only about 4000 years ago, probably by visiting Asian seafarers. Dingoes became part of Aboriginal life, helping them to hunt game and keeping them warm as 'living blankets' on cold nights. These wild dogs spread throughout the mainland; hunting alone or in packs, they ate whatever they could catch, including native mammals, which were therefore doomed to extinction. They also took sheep and cattle, which led to the construction of the world's longest fence, the dingo fence, which runs 5000 km (3000 miles) from Queensland to South Australia, intended to keep dingoes out of the farmlands of the southeast.

Nowadays the dingo itself is endangered – persecuted for attacking farm animals, but also vanishing as a species through interbreeding with domestic dogs. However, pure-bred dingoes can still be seen trotting through the spinifex grasslands of the vast arid interior, their howling calls drifting across the wilderness.

1. Barrow Island euros (a kind of kangaroo) shelter from the heat of the sun under the machinery of an oil installation. This subspecies is found nowhere else.

ISLAND SANCTUARY

An oilfield might seem like a hostile place to live. Luffkins, huge nodding pumps, hiss and sweat to draw oil from deep underground and huge pits of gas burn like furnaces on an already sweltering day. Between termite mounds and spinifex grass, great bundles of pipelines are draped across the red landscape. It is hard to believe that such a place could also be a sanctuary for some of Australia's most rare and endangered animals.

Barrow Island, off the coast of Western Australia, was declared a Class-A nature reserve in 1910 because of its wealth of wildlife. Fourteen species of mammals live here, and more than 100 bird species. It was also considered as a potential British nuclear testing site in the 1950s, but this was not pursued. However, large quantities of oil were discovered on the island in 1954, too much to

ignore, so a way had to be found to reconcile its natural and economic importance.

It's the largest landmass in Australia, and possibly the world, with no introduced rats or mice, but more importantly it has no foxes. The oil company based here now takes conservation very seriously and strict quarantine rules keep out introduced animals and diseases. In spite of the heavy industry, wildlife finds sanctuary on this island and some of the species are found almost nowhere else. The golden bandicoot, a small, long-nosed marsupial, was once widespread all across inland Australia. Now it is virtually extinct on the mainland, but 50,000 thrive on Barrow Island. Similarly, the burrowing bettong, also called the boodie, hangs on by a thread elsewhere, existing only as wild populations on four islands. Barrow has a thriving population of these marsupials, which look like miniature, round-eared kangaroos, and

The endangered Gippsland earthworm, unique to Victoria, grows 1 m (over 3 feet) long and 2 cm (almost an inch) in diameter. Not much is known about it, but it is said to make a gurgling noise as it moves underground.

1

they hop about the oil-workers' accommodation blocks at night, hiding in sandy burrows by day.

Perenties, Australia's largest lizards, which grow up to 2 m (6 feet 6 inches) long, crawl around the islands, sheltering under huts and sipping from dripping water pipes. The Barrow Island euro, a kind of kangaroo, is also common here. On hot days, groups gather in the shade of oil installations and have to be deterred from sitting underneath moving machinery. They can often be found resting on the seashore. Three species of marine turtle come ashore to lay their eggs on the island's beaches, and white-bellied sea eagles nest on the island too.

No-one has hunted on Barrow Island for thousands of years, so many of the animals are bold and trusting. Oil workers have to be reminded not to feed them, but at night a barbecue will draw them in anyway. As burrowing bettongs hop around the barbie looking for scraps, it's hard to believe that they are an endangered species.

Australia has thousands of islands around its huge coastline, and many of them are now important conservation areas. Without them, nine further species of mammal would almost certainly be extinct. While introduced predators roam the mainland, these islands are vital refuges for animals that often have nowhere else to go.

 BRAND NEW FROG

Incredible as it may seem, new species of animals are being found in Australia even today. In the peat swamps of the far southwest of Western Australia, in the summer of 1994, a frog was discovered that was like no other. Measuring 35 mm (1½ inches) long, it had a blue and white belly and its legs, hands and throat were bright orange, so it was given the name 'sunset frog'. It was described for science only in 1997.

The sunset frog seems to belong to a very ancient line of frogs, which has lived in splendid isolation for millions of years in this tiny moist corner of the country. It lays its eggs singly in small pools of water, but little is yet known of the tadpoles or how they grow up.

The frogs are known only from a few dozen sites, and because of their low numbers and tiny range there is a fear they will disappear into extinction, but not enough is known about them to predict their future. What is astonishing is that the frog was found in an area that was really not out of the way; scientists had thought they knew the wildlife of the region pretty well. In this enormous country, what other hidden secrets might there be?

1. Golden bandicoots, almost extinct on the mainland, thrive in a predator-free island haven. Turtle eggs laid on the island's beaches are a seasonal meal.

2. (opposite) Quokkas are rare on the mainland, but common on Rottnest Island off Perth, where they are safe from foxes.

Overleaf: Green turtles come ashore to Barrow Island's beaches to lay their eggs.

WILDLIFE LOST AND FOUND

At the far southwestern corner of Western Australia is a beautiful and remote location called Two Peoples Bay. It is an area of heathland overlooking the Southern Ocean, and in spring it is full of wildflowers and birds. One bird call is distinctively loud and has the odd characteristic of seeming to come from several different directions at once. It's the song of the noisy scrub-bird, described by the 19th-century naturalist John Gilbert as the loudest of all the songbirds he knew. But by the beginning of the 20th century this little brown bird with tiny wings was becoming increasingly elusive, and eventually it seemed to have vanished altogether.

However, in 1961, a local schoolteacher spotted one and then a few more were found in the area. Great efforts were made to protect its habitat, the birds were reintroduced to other sites and numbers began to increase. The future looked much rosier. And then, another astonishing discovery was made.

A little hopping marsupial called Gilbert's potoroo had once thrived in the same place as the noisy scrub-bird. The size of a small rabbit, it emerged at night to search for truffles in the heathland. It hadn't been seen for over 100 years and was presumed long extinct. Then, in 1994, one was found by chance in Two Peoples Bay. Here was another animal that hadn't died out after all. The tiny remnant population was carefully monitored, and animals have been brought into captivity in an intensive effort to save the species. The

numbers are still not high and, with only a few dozen animals known to be alive, it is possibly the rarest mammal in Australia and critically endangered, but it is not extinct.

There are many such examples of animals sadly added to the 'extinct' list, but then rediscovered. In the wet tropical woodlands of northern Queensland lives a gliding marsupial, the mahogany glider, which 'flies' from tree to tree on flaps of skin stretched between its limbs. But trees began to vanish as settlers cleared the forest to plant bananas and sugar cane. Described for science as recently as 1883, by 1886 the mahogany glider was becoming difficult to find. In fact there were doubts as to whether it had ever existed at all as a separate species. For a while it was thought to be identical to the much commoner squirrel glider, but in the 1980s

some stuffed animals were found tucked away and forgotten in a museum drawer. One had been collected as recently as 1974. Scientists were now able to establish that it was a distinct species after all and finally, in 1989, living mahogany gliders were found in the wild. Again, it's an animal that is still in difficulties; its home is prime farmland and 80 per cent of its former habitat is under cultivation.

The mountain pygmy possum has an even stranger story. The size of a mouse, this little possum was a real mystery for 70 years. No European had ever set eyes on a living one – it was known only from fossilized remains, 15,000 years old, found in caves. As far as anyone knew, it was not only extinct, it was ancient history. However, in 1966, a living animal was found in a ski hut in the chilly alpine area of Victoria. The mountain pygmy

2

3

possum lives only in the southern mountains of Australia, a landscape covered in snow for months of the year, and it spends the winter in hibernation. Skiers had apparently seen these animals before, but assumed they were mice.

How can animals stay lost like this? Australia is a big country, and even today it is full of inaccessible and barely inhabited regions. Many animals are in tiny, fragmented populations and some may be in danger of disappearing even before they can be redis-covered. But some 'lost' species are being found with the help of those who know the country best.

The great desert skink is a large lizard. Growing up to 40 cm (16 inches) long, and red in colour, it is quite distinctive. It was first recorded from the Great Victoria Desert of

Western Australia in the 1890s, but subse-quent reports of it were few and far between. Although scientists searched in earnest, only a handful of these big lizards were found in 100 years. But then a faded museum specimen was shown to a group of Aboriginal people in remote Western Australia and some older members of the community recognized it immediately. It was an animal they hunted, and it was also important to them as a 'law', or spiritual, creature, so they knew where to look for it in the vast landscape in which it lived.

Now Aboriginal communities and scien-tists are joining forces to find this elusive lizard, share knowledge of its behaviour and habitat, and work out ways to help it survive. This combination of ancient wisdom and modern science may be its saviour.

1. Gilbert's potoroo was once thought to be extinct, but a handful have been rediscovered. It lives a secretive life and feeds on almost nothing but truffles.

2. Two Peoples Bay, in the far southwest of Australia, is home to Gilbert's potoroo.

3. Mountain pygmy possums live among boulders high in the mountains of south-eastern Australia, waking from winter hibernation to feed on migrating moths.

1. Kangaroo Island still has large areas of its original native vegetation – valuable habitat for a wealth of wildlife.

2. The Kangaroo Island kangaroo is a subspecies of the mainland western grey kangaroo.

3. A pair of Cape Barren geese share nest duties. The eggs are laid in a cup-shaped nest of rough grass.

Overleaf: The diminutive tammar wallaby has vanished from many areas of the southern mainland, where it was once widespread, but it is still abundant on Kangaroo Island.

1

KANGAROO ISLAND

There is a wonderful island for wildlife within an hour's ferry trip of Adelaide. It is a place of wild beaches, extensive woodlands and strange rocks, but it is also criss-crossed with roads and there are towns, farms and an airport. It is not a remote wilderness and yet it has an astonishing range of wildlife, including some rare and endangered animals no longer found on the mainland. This is Kangaroo Island, the third largest island off Australia's coast.

It was first visited by Europeans in 1802, who found a wilderness with unusual animals. There were extraordinarily tame kangaroos and seals on the shore that didn't seem nervous of people. There was also a large number of short-legged dwarf emus, which so intrigued one French explorer that he captured a couple to take back to the French empress Josephine. But sealers and kangaroo hunters soon moved into this idyll. The dwarf emu was hunted to extinction within 50 years and Kangaroo Island was being affected by European settlement just as the mainland was.

By the late 19th century some people were beginning to realize the value of Australia's wild places and, as early as 1892, conservationists struggled to get a part of Kangaroo Island saved from being cleared for agriculture. They finally succeeded, and now half of the island still has its original native vegetation. There are thick swathes of coastal mallee eucalypts and heathland remaining here, the like of which has mostly been cleared from the mainland.

In the 1920s conservationists went a step further. Fearing that some animals were in danger of disappearing from the mainland,

2

3

they decided to bring them to Kangaroo Island for safety. They shipped over koalas and platypus, a wombat, some mallee fowl, possums, emus, various doves, Cape Barren geese, another wombat and some tortoises. This strange, haphazard assortment had mixed fortunes – some species didn't survive, but others prospered. Cape Barren geese, once in danger of extinction, thrive here, raising their young in grassy nests on the ground, but they remain among the world's rarest native geese. Koalas, which are not native to the island, did so well that they were, and still are, in danger of eating the trees bare of gum leaves.

Native animals do especially well here because, once again, that are no dingoes, rabbits or foxes. People tried to introduce the latter two in the 1800s, but fortunately they failed and the difference that makes is enormous. Tiny tammar wallabies once lived in great numbers on the South Australian mainland before introduced grazers and predators saw them off, but on Kangaroo Island they are still abundant, grazing at the edge of roads and even venturing into town on summer nights looking for food. The bird life, too, is strikingly varied. Glossy black cockatoos, a subspecies extinct on the South

Australian mainland, nest here in tree hollows. Fairy penguins, the world's smallest, come in noisily each evening from the sea to their burrows on the wild beaches, with no fear of attack from foxes, just as they did long before any European set foot on the island.

There have been enormous changes in the last two centuries since European settlement and, while many animals are struggling, others have adapted and thrived. When given a chance, the native wildlife is resilient because it is at home here, having evolved to live in the unique and unpredictable land-scapes of this island continent.

GAZETTEER

The authors travelled to all corners of Australasia to research and film the most beautiful landscapes and exciting wildlife while making the *Wild Down Under* television series on which this book is based. These are their personal choices of the very best places to experience the natural wonders of the region.

RAINFORESTS

Tropical Rainforests, Queensland

① Daintree

The Daintree region has some of the most beautiful and easily accessible tropical rainforest found anywhere on Earth. The combination of forest trees, climbing vines and fan palms give it a character all of its own. Daintree National Park is just a two-hour drive north of Cairns on a sealed road and within a day you can explore the forest from a variety of excellent boardwalks as well as from a canopy tower at the Daintree Environmental Centre. You'll see or hear a fantastic range of birds, often including Victoria's riflebird, wompoo pigeons, catbirds, cassowary, brush

turkeys and yellow-footed scrub fowl. Join one of the many local wildlife tours and you stand a good chance of spotting ringtail and striped possums, Bennett's tree kangaroos and musky rat kangaroos. Tours of the Daintree River take you into crocodile territory, and at certain times of year thousands of spectacled flying foxes camp close to its banks, providing a spectacular fly-out at dusk. The most comfortable time to visit is during the dry season, from May to October, but the area is generally accessible throughout the year.

② Atherton Tablelands

A short drive inland from Cairns up a spectacular escarpment brings you to a whole variety of easily accessible rainforest locations. Alternatively, ascend the escarpment on the Cairns-to-Kuranda skyrail, a cable car that provides one of the best views in the world of a rainforest canopy. On the tableland itself, Lakes Eacham and Barrine are beautiful crater lakes surrounded by forest. Duck-billed platypus are common in the streams here. Nearby, just beside the road at Yungaburra, the curtain fig is an extraordinary botanical sight, a huge strangler fig that has fallen over and then grown a massive, cascading curtain of roots.

③ Cape York

A four-wheel-drive trip to Cape York during the dry season (it's mostly inaccessible in the wet) is a true adventure for wildlife-watchers. The rainforests of Iron Range National Park contain many animals that are found in New Guinea but not elsewhere in Queensland, such as grey and spotted cuscus, eclectus parrots and the spectacular black palm cockatoos. An added bonus of a trip to the rainforests of Cape York is that you will also pass through wonderful tropical savannah with a completely different collection of wildlife.

④ Eungella National Park

This area of subtropical rainforest is largely wilderness and relatively inaccessible, but the viewing platform on the Broken River is one of the best places in all Australia to observe the duck-billed platypus. Dawn and dusk are best; waiting silently at these times is often rewarded with a view of this extraordinary creature.

⑤ Lamington National Park

This is another wonderful area of subtropical rainforest and other vegetation types too, just over 100 km (60 miles) south of Brisbane. Easy walks make this an accessible location; the bird-watching is fantastic and wildlife highlights include Albert's lyrebird and red-legged pademelons. There is also a rainforest canopy walkway at Green Mountains.

For further information on all Queensland parks visit the Queensland Parks and Wildlife Service at www.epa.qld.gov.au/environment/park/discover and for travel www.destinationqueensland.com

Cool Rainforests, Tasmania

⑥ Franklin-Gordon Wild Rivers National Park

This is a fabulous wilderness of rainforest and mountains, waterfalls, streams and rivers and there are many ways to experience it. For the adventurous there are hiking trails, such as the one to Frenchman's Cap Mountain, or white-water rafting down the Franklin. Both take several days to complete and carry you into the heart of the wilderness. At the other end of the scale you can take an air-conditioned cruise boat out of Strahan on the west coast for a wonderful trip up the majestic Gordon River, surrounded by lush forest, with a short rainforest walk included

RAINFORESTS

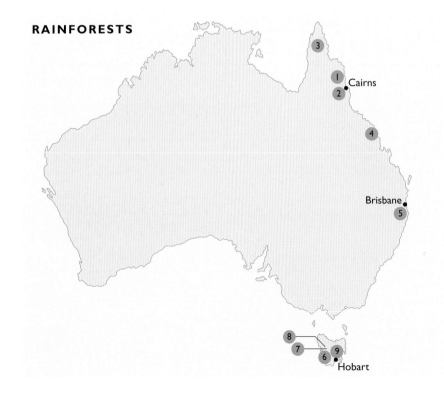

1. A snowy scene in Smoko Creek, Tasmania

at Heritage Landing. The Lyell Highway from Lake St Clair to Queenstown passes through the park and has a variety of beautiful viewpoints, as well as short scenic walks through forest to streams, waterfalls and lookouts.

7 Lake St Clair

This lake is Australia's deepest and is surrounded by a fascinating mosaic of temperate rainforest and eucalypts, with snow gums and cushion plants at higher elevations. For a good overview take a boat trip on the lake. Platypus Bay, a short walk from the visitor centre, is an excellent location for spotting platypus at dusk and echidnas are also common on these paths. Day walks to Shadow and Forgotten Lakes take you up through rainforest into alpine scenery. For a real challenge there is the Overland Track, which ends here after a four- or five-day hike from Cradle Mountain, past Tasmania's tallest peaks. As an added bonus, cute little eastern quolls shelter in some of the huts along the way. They are very bold, picking up scraps from hikers.

8 Cradle Mountain

A real mecca for wildlife, this area has some of the most stunning scenery in Tasmania. There is a variety of short and longer walks through alpine rainforest, across button-grass plains, around beautiful alpine lakes, and all with the magnificent rocky peak of Cradle Mountain itself in the background. From the roadside you'll see Bennett's wallabies and Tasmanian pademelons

during the day and maybe even a brush-tailed possum around the lodge. If you drive from the park HQ to Dove Lake at night you'll also have a good chance of seeing many wombats and possums, and if you're lucky a Tasmanian devil or eastern quoll. In the winter, snow falls from time to time and if the roads remain open this is one of the best places in Australia to watch wallabies and wombats in snowy scenery.

9 Mount Field

This park is just 78 km (49 miles) from Hobart, so easily accessible in a day trip. With a mixture of rainforest, subalpine forest and high moorland and good walks, this is also a great introduction to Tasmania's wild areas. Bennett's wallabies and Tasmanian pademelons hang around the picnic areas and if you camp overnight you are likely to see many more mammals too. In autumn, from April to mid-May, the leaves of the southern beech trees turn a stunning orange colour before falling and many people come to view this. When it snows there is also cross-country and downhill skiing.

For further information on all Tasmanian wildlife and travel visit www.parks.tas.gov.au and www.discovertasmania.com.au

DESERTS

10 Sturt National Park, New South Wales

In the far northwest corner of New South Wales, Sturt's rocky plains, sand dunes and flat-topped breakaway hills with green river valleys are a haven for red kangaroos, emus, colourful parrots and wedge-tailed eagles. Once a large cattle station, the park retains the dams that provide vital water to its wildlife. One of the best times to visit is early spring, when it's not too hot and a bit of rain may have brought out colourful wildflowers. During a drive around the park you'll be amazed by the number of big red kangaroos with their playful joeys; male emus with striped chicks striding out in search of food; and odd-looking shingle-backed lizards crossing the road. Spend a morning or evening at one of the dams to see a parade of kangaroos, emus, birds and dingoes. Large flocks of white corellas, pretty little cockatiels and green budgerigars are easily spotted. It's a big park with some great camping sites. The nearby town of Tibooburra has food, fuel and accommodation, and a NSW Parks Office and Information Centre.

For further information visit www.nationalparks.nsw.gov.au and www.visitnsw.com.au

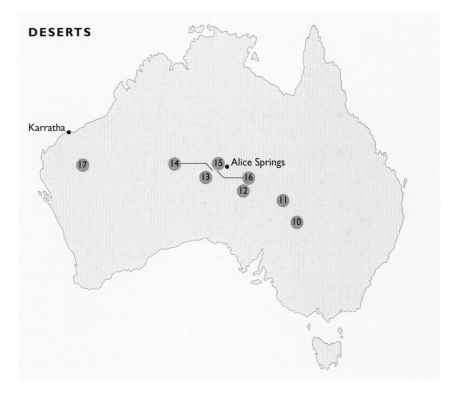

DESERTS

Karratha

Alice Springs

11 Innamincka Regional Reserve, South Australia

The lakes and swamps of Innamincka create an important wetland in the searing desert. They fill via the Cooper Creek, which carries seasonal pulses of water into the centre from wetter areas of Queensland. River red gums and coolibahs line waterholes and lakes rich in fish and aquatic life attract a multitude of water birds – at least 20,000 live around Coongie Lake throughout the year. Every tree near a waterhole can be a mass of cormorants, snake-necked darters, spoonbills and rufous herons; while coots, ducks and pelicans bob around on the surface. The adjacent land is important for frogs and many small mammals such as dunnarts and planigales, which shelter in cracks in the soil. Red kangaroos, emus and dingoes are also common, and keep your eye out for snakes. This area can become impassable with floods, so check with South Australia Parks before planning a visit and to arrange a visitor's pass. The small town of Innamincka has a ranger's office, accommodation, food and fuel.

For further information visit www.environment.sa.gov.au/parks

12 Witjira National Park and Dalhousie Mound Springs, South Australia

On the western edge of the Simpson Desert is a true oasis – Dalhousie Springs. Vast quantities of artesian water bubble up from the ground to form large warm pools and flowing creeks. Tall reeds, bulrushes and melaleucas surround the pools, sheltering variegated wrens, swallows and mudlarks. A variety of unique fish lives in the warm water, as well as other aquatic life. Large date palms, planted by cameleers as they travelled the old trade route though the centre, grow on many of the mound springs. The springs are also an important archaeological site, as Aboriginal people lived around the permanent water for thousands of years. A wonderful way to appreciate the wildlife is to sit in the warm main pool, watching ducks and coots glide over the water, as galahs and dingoes come to drink. From the springs it's a short drive to the first dunes of the Simpson Desert and Purnie Bore, a man-made wetland. When the spinifex is seeding, millions of zebra finches flock to this water to relieve their thirst. The road continues east across hundreds of the Simpson's dunes to Birdsville, a trek for experienced four-wheel drivers only and not to be tackled in summer. You can camp at Dalhousie; a park ranger is resident and you will need a Desert

1

Parks pass from South Australia Parks and Wildlife, who have a comprehensive website at www.environment.sa.gov.au/parks

13 Uluru–Kata Tjuta National Park, Northern Territory

This park is accessible by paved road or, alternatively, you can fly here. It has its own accommodation village, Yulara, so it is one of the easiest places in the desert to visit. While the wildlife is abundant, most people come to see Uluru (Ayers Rock), the most famous rock in the world, but are often surprised to discover that Kata Tjuta (the Olgas), with its 36 orange domes and secret valleys, can be more impressive. The park is a World Heritage Area, recognized for its natural and cultural importance. This is a special area for Aboriginal people, the Anangu, and you can learn about its significance at the wonderful Cultural Centre. The Anangu conduct tours of the park, and it's on the route of most central Australian tour operators. You can also take a scenic flight by small plane or helicopter.

For further information visit www.ea.gov.au/parks/uluru

14 Kings Canyon, Northern Territory

To the north of Uluru–Kata Tjuta is Watarrka National Park, with its famous Kings Canyon. This canyon has sheer walls reaching up 200 m (650 feet) from Kings Creek. It is an easy walk up the boulder-strewn creek bed under the shade of grevilleas, wattles and eucalypts, which are rich in parrots, honey-eaters and other birds. A spectacular 6-km (4-mile) walk takes you up into amazing red 'beehive' rock formations and around the rim of the canyon. Walkers are rewarded with wonderful views of the sandstone range and distant spinifexed sand plains dotted

with desert oak. Falcons roost on the canyon walls and fairy martins make mud nests in sheltered crevices. Rock wallabies and larger euros can be seen during the evenings, feeding on grassy slopes. The canyon is also famous for its deep, secluded Garden of Eden gorge with its permanent waterholes, a refuge for relict plants such as delicate ferns and huge cycads.

15 MacDonnell Ranges and Ormiston Gorge, Northern Territory

Alice Springs is the gateway to most of central Australia and lies in the middle of the stunning MacDonnell Ranges – over 400 km (250 miles) of rocky peaks, sheltered gorges with permanent waterholes, sandy riverbeds, wildlife-rich woodlands and Aboriginal heritage. One of the most spectacular sites is Ormiston Gorge in the western Macs. This is one of the best places to watch black-footed rock wallabies feeding on the gorge cliffs, chasing one another or coming to the waterhole to drink. Fish live in the waters of the gorge and kites can be seen skimming the surface, grabbing fish in their talons. A variety of parrots lives in river red gums, as do butcherbirds, mudlarks and crows, and western bowerbirds build their bowers amongst the mulga scrub. Dingoes are also common. You can camp at Ormiston; park rangers live here and conduct informative talks, and there is an information office.

16 Palm Valley, Northern Territory

The magnificent, lush Palm Valley is a leisurely two-hour drive to the west of Alice Springs. The final 20 km (12 miles) are a great experience, as you drive along the mostly dry Finke River, then on a very bumpy track to the valley itself. Over 1000 cabbage palms and cycads are set amongst ancient red cliffs, rock amphitheatres and hills. They are the relatives of rainforest plants that

1. Beautiful Ormiston Gorge in the Northern Territory: one of the best places to see some of the desert's wildlife.

2. Noisy, colourful galahs are often seen at waterholes in the desert.

2

covered Australia 65 million years ago. Between the stands of palms are reedy pools of water that seeps out of the sandstone. Beautiful white ghost gums grow out of the steep rock walls and cypress pines add extra greenery. It is an easy walk through the valley and the track loops back over a flat ridge, providing some great views. The main valley of palms is accessible only by four-wheel-drive. Various tour operators visit Palm Valley, which is part of Finke Gorge National Park.

For further information on all Northern Territory desert parks visit www.nt.gov.au/ipe/pwcnt and www.alicesprings.nt.gov.au/tourism

17 Karijini National Park, Western Australia

This is a remote and beautiful park in the harsh Pilbara region, half a day's drive from the coastal town of Karratha. It is famous for its spectacular gorges, which plunge vertically into the spinifex-covered hills, slicing down through layers of red rock several billion years old. There are a number of high viewpoints, but the best way to experience these geological wonders is to descend into their narrow and twisting depths. Some have well-made paths to broad swimming holes, such as Fortescue Falls, but others, such as Weano and Joffre Gorges, narrow down to a metre or two (3–6 feet) wide and need some scrambling to reach the most scenic parts. You have to take care not to go too far and get lost or shoot down a waterfall up which it is impossible to return – every year people have to be rescued. There is an excellent visitor centre and several campsites in the park, but no food or water is available. The nearest small town is Tom Price, an hour outside the park. Karijini is easiest to visit in the dry season, from April to November.

For further information visit www.calm.wa.gov.au/national_parks or email Karratha Tourist Bureau at tourist.bureau@kisser.net.au

GUM TREE COUNTRY

18 Barmah Forest and Murray River, Victoria

About three hours' drive north from Melbourne, this is a marvellously atmospheric eucalypt forest of river red gums, right on the edge of the mighty Murray River. It's the biggest area of red gum forest left and some of the trees are 500 years old, gnarled and full of holes. The classic Australian animals can be seen here – kookaburras, koalas, kangaroos and emus. Birdlife is rich, and spring and early summer are the best times to visit. You might spot a superb parrot, a rare and beautiful long-tailed bird, high in the trees near its nest-hole, and at the river's edge you'll see herons, spoonbills and a range of other water birds. The forest is easy to walk in, and there are camping grounds. But don't camp right under a red gum – they drop their branches very suddenly! The Murray's waters are now under tight human control, but every few years in spring the water is allowed to flow into the trees, creating a flooded forest.

19 Yarra Ranges National Park, Victoria

Victoria is the home of the world's tallest hardwood tree, the mountain ash. These trees are so massive you feel completely dwarfed by them. The forests here are lush and green, with impressive tree ferns and dense, damp undergrowth. The Yarra Ranges have many old and huge trees. By day there's plenty of birdsong, including the duetting of whipbirds. It's also worth waiting for evening, because after dark the forest has a different character – from hollows in the huge, dark trees possums emerge and make lots of noise as they start their night's feeding. Mountain brush-tail possums clamber to the ground to forage about or feed on fruiting trees, and you might see a greater glider up in the trees. As night falls, bats flit about and owl calls start up, with the boobook's call imitating its own name.

20 Kinglake National Park, Victoria

Northwest of the Yarra Ranges, this is another area of very tall trees. Kinglake is also a key place to view one of the wildlife specialities of the area, the superb lyrebird. Try the Jehosaphat Gully and Masons Falls picnic areas, where you may spot a male displaying just off the walking track. Brightly coloured rosellas are also easy to see here.

For further information on all Victorian parks visit www.parkweb.vic.gov.au

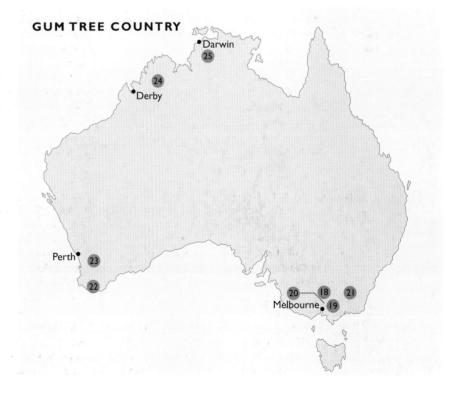

GUM TREE COUNTRY

Darwin
25

24

Derby

Perth
23

22

20 — 18   21
Melbourne   19

1

21 Kosciuszko National Park, New South Wales

This mountainous park, which contains the highest peak in Australia, has stunning landscapes that change dramatically through the seasons. Visit in summer and you'll find the alpine area carpeted by flowers, with red-necked and swamp wallabies living among the snow gums. In winter the landscape is transformed: the softly rounded mountains are covered in deep snow, and cross-country and downhill skiing take over from walking. The rugged snow gums, the only trees to grow at this high altitude, are striking when they're covered in snow and ice. Most animals move to lower ground in winter, but wombats may still be seen trundling around. Access is more difficult in the winter, so check local road conditions.

For further information visit
www.nationalparks.nsw.gov.au

22 Valley of the Giants, Western Australia

Western Australia is home to some extraordinary eucalypts. Among them is the huge red tingle tree, and the Valley of the Giants near Walpole (420 km/260 miles southeast of Perth) is the place to see them. In this forest, which has a very ancient feel, these eucalypts grow 16m (over 50 feet) in circumference, and some hollow ones are big enough to walk around inside! But the best way to see these stately trees is from the Treetop Walk, an easy but dramatic walkway through the tree canopy that rises to 40m (130 feet) above the ground. This puts you eye to eye with birdlife: you might see purple-crowned lorikeets, pardalotes and treecreepers flying and feeding. The area is open all year.

23 Dryandra Woodland, Western Australia

This beautiful piece of open eucalypt woodland, one of the last remnants in this area of wheat farming, is a very special place. It's a three-hour drive southeast of Perth on good roads and is a wonderful place to see some of southwestern Australia's native wildlife, including some endangered species. The rare and exquisite little numbat has found a refuge here, and it's possible to see them feeding on termites on sunny mornings. Shingleback lizards bask on the paths between the trees, and kangaroos are around early in the morning. Many of the animals emerge only after dark, and this is the time to go 'spotlighting' – looking for wildlife by torchlight. You might see brush-tailed bettongs, brush-tail possums and tammar wallabies. There is basic overnight accommodation and the best time to visit is during spring, from September to November, to view numbats and woodland flowers.

24 The Kimberley Gorges, Western Australia

The Kimberley region, in the far northwest, is one of the most remote parts of Australia, and Windjana and Geikie Gorges and Tunnel Creek are among the country's most dramatic landscapes. Windjana Gorge is cut through by the fast-flowing Lennard River in the wet season, but in the dry it retreats to pools in the deep gorge. This is the time to visit – take a short walk along the gorge to see freshwater crocodiles in the pools or basking on the sandbanks. There are fruit bats living in the gorge that fly out along the gorge at dusk, and noisy flocks of corellas, too. Tunnel Creek, which is nearby, is quite an experience – the creek flows through a tunnel 750 m (2500 feet) long and it is possible to walk right through it, although you'll need a torch and a bit of nerve. There are pools of water on the ground to wade through, with bats and sometimes freshwater crocodiles.

Geikie Gorge has the mighty Fitzroy River flowing through it. You can take a pleasant walk along its banks or a guided boat trip. The gorge is cut through a massive coral reef, 300 million years old, and you can still see the fossilized corals in the walls.

Windjana Gorge is two hours' drive from Derby, with Tunnel Creek 30 km (20 miles) further on. Geikie Gorge is a short drive from Fitzroy Crossing.

For further information on all Western Australian parks visit www.calm.wa.gov.au/national_parks and for travel in the Kimberley region www.kimberleytourism.com

25 Kakadu National Park, Northern Territory

Kakadu, in the far north of the Northern Territory, is one of Australia's wildlife jewels and should not be missed. The landscape of rocky escarpments, wetlands and woodlands is stunning, and there's an enormous range of wildlife. Frilled lizards and antilopine wallaroos can be seen by day around the eucalypt woodlands, and a host of animals emerge after dark – you might catch bandicoots and sugar gliders in the beam of a spotlight, and hear the assorted calls of night birds. A boat trip on Yellow Water is a fantastic way to see a host of wildlife; very early morning is the best time to experience this. The birdlife is spectacular: magpie geese, storks, jacanas and sea eagles are easy to see. Saltwater crocodiles swim past very close and haul themselves out onto the banks. There is more than can be seen in one day; the ancient rock paintings at Ubirr and Nourlangie are fascinating and easily reached, and there are beautiful waterfalls that tumble over the escarpment (although they stop flowing during the dry season). Kakadu is about a three-hour drive from Darwin along good roads, although flooding can occasionally be a problem in the wet season, between November and April. Any time in the dry season, from May to October, is good but birdlife is most impressive later in the season when the waterholes are more crowded.

For further information visit
www.ea.gov.au/parks/kakadu

1. Birds flying over Kakadu National Park during the wet season.

2. Australian pelicans live on the beaches of Shark Bay, Western Australia.

OCEANS

26 Great Barrier Reef, Queensland

The Great Barrier Reef offers many fantastic opportunities to experience some of the best coral reefs in the world. On this vast reef system there is everything from gentle snorkelling to wilderness diving, so the only problem is knowing where to start. In the south there are a number of islands right on the reef on which you can stay. Heron Island is reached by ferry or helicopter from Gladstone, and Lady Elliott Island has a short airstrip for regular flights from the Queensland coast. Both have some of the best coral on the entire reef, so there is stunning snorkelling and diving. They are also great places to see turtles and manta rays. For a more remote experience, and a chance to see the outer reefs, there are many live-aboard diving boats departing from Cairns and Port Douglas. With the luxury of several days at sea you can explore some of the more pristine reefs, such as the Ribbon Reefs off Cooktown, the Great Detached Reef and Raine Island even further north. All these locations have breathtaking walls and spectacular drop-offs which attract the big pelagic fish such as tuna, trevally and sharks. Day trips from Port Douglas are one of the quickest ways to experience the reef for a few hours.

For further information on travel to the reef visit www.destinationqueensland.com

27 Whale Sharks at Ningaloo Reef, Western Australia

Ningaloo is *the* place to see whale sharks, the largest fish in the sea. Boat cruises work with spotter planes to give people the unforgettable experience of swimming alongside whale sharks and manta rays. The remote town of Exmouth, 1300 km (800 miles) north of Perth, is the gateway to Ningaloo. Whale-shark tours depart from here and from the smaller town of Coral Bay, 150 km (100 miles) to the south. The great attraction of Ningaloo Reef is its proximity to the mainland, and from Coral Bay you can snorkel over beautiful coral gardens within a few metres of the shore. The best time for snorkelling and diving at Ningaloo is between April and November and the whale-shark season is from mid-March to June.

For further information on Ningaloo Marine Park visit www.calm.wa.gov.au/national_parks and also www.westernaustralia.net/discover/gascoyne

28 Shark Bay, Western Australia

This is one of the best places in Australia to see dugongs, dolphins and turtles. At the small resort of Monkey Mia on the shores of Shark Bay a few well-known dolphins come to the beach to accept hand-outs of fish. Every day, rangers manage the interactions, selecting people from the crowd to wade forward and hand-feed the dolphins. Wildlife-watching boats also depart from Monkey Mia to sail the waters of Shark Bay, where sightings of dolphins in a more natural setting are guaranteed. It is also possible to see herds of dugongs, green and loggerhead turtles, sea snakes and some of the many shark species that lend their name to the bay. You can feed the dolphins and see the wildlife all year round, but for the best weather visit between June and October. Shark Bay is 800 km (500 miles) north of Perth, so allow a couple of days to drive there; alternatively, there are direct flights from Perth several times a week.

For further information on Shark Bay visit www.calm.wa.gov.au/national_parks and for Monkey Mia www.monkeymia.com.au

Dolphin-watching

There are many locations around Australia where you can see and interact with wild dolphins. Rockingham and Bunbury 29, both within two hours' drive of Perth, offer the chance to swim with these graceful creatures. Melbourne's Port Phillip Bay 30 and Moreton Bay 31 close to Brisbane have regular boat trips to see dolphins,

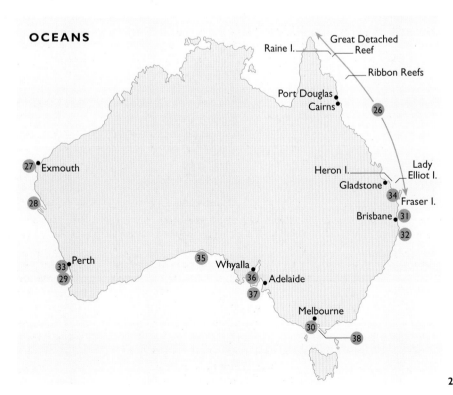

OCEANS

Raine I. — Great Detached Reef
Ribbon Reefs
Port Douglas
Cairns
26
Exmouth 27
28
Heron I.
Gladstone
Lady Elliot I.
34 Fraser I.
Brisbane 31
32
Perth 33
35
Whyalla
29
36 Adelaide
37
Melbourne
30
38

2

1

and look out for dolphins surfing the waves off Byron Bay ③② , in northern New South Wales.

For further information on Bunbury Dolphins visit www.dolphindiscovery.com.au and for Rockingham Dolphins www.dolphins.com.au

㉝ Rottnest Island, Western Australia

The specialities of Rottnest Island are the quokkas, little rabbit-sized wallabies found only in Western Australia. This is one of their last refuges, but they thrive here in their thousands and are not shy. As well as quokka-watching, Rottnest is marvellous for birds, too – coastal birds include ospreys, terns, shearwaters and rock parrots, and around inland lakes there are sandpipers and avocets, among others. Rottnest Island is a very popular weekend tourist spot, with its blue waters and white beaches. It's only an hour's ferry ride from Perth.

For further information visit www.westernaustralia.net/discover/perth/rottnest

Whale-watching

Few wildlife-watching experiences are as overwhelming as an encounter with a great whale, and Australia has some of the world's best whale-watching opportunities. The east and west coasts are highways for thousands of migrating humpback and southern right whales. Queensland's Hervey Bay ㉞ , near Frazer Island, is the best spot on the east coast to see humpbacks and their calves. You can see whales almost every day from August to mid-October – tour boats depart from the Urangan Boat Harbour. The Head of the Bight

㉟ , 1000 km (625 miles) west of Adelaide, is the biggest calving area for southern right whales and offers some of the world's best land-based whale-watching. Looking down from the cliff-tops you can see whales from May to October, with the peak in July and August.

For further information visit www.hervey.com.au for humpbacks at Hervey Bay, and www.environment.sa.gov.au/parks/whales for southern right whales in South Australia.

㊱ Giant Australian Cuttlefish, Whyalla, South Australia

Whyalla, about 400 km (250 miles) northwest of Adelaide, is the cuttlefish capital of the world. Every year millions of giant Australian cuttlefish congregate in its waters in one of Australia's greatest underwater spectacles. Between May and August they gather on rocky reefs to breed; some of the best locations are in shallow water and easily accessible from the shore. The cuttlefish are unconcerned by people in the water, so whether snorkelling or diving you can get literally within centimetres of these spectacular animals. Cuttlefish are among the most charismatic creatures in the ocean, so the opportunity to see such a vast number of them in one place is not to be missed. Local tour operators run trips.

For further information visit www.cuttlefishcapital.com.au

㊲ Kangaroo Island, South Australia

A short ferry ride from Cape Jervis, south of Adelaide, Kangaroo Island is one of the best

places to see, without too much difficulty, a guaranteed range of wildlife. Seal Bay is home to about 700 Australian sea lions. Adults haul ashore on the sandy beaches to rest after long fishing trips and the pups spend their time either sleeping or playing. There is a boardwalk where you can watch them from a distance, or you can join one of the guided tours along the beach for a closer view of these endearing animals. There's also a whole range of land-based wildlife. Little tammar wallabies are abundant, as are Cape Barren geese. Koalas were introduced and are now here in large numbers (rather too many, as they're stripping the trees), making them very easy to see. Echidnas can be seen walking along roadsides. The birdlife is also superb, with many rare species including glossy black cockatoos and beautiful fire-tails.

For further information visit www.environment.sa.gov.au/parks

㊳ Penguin Parade, Phillip Island, Victoria

Phillip Island Nature Park is home to one of Australia's most popular wildlife attractions, the Penguin Parade. Every night at sunset hundreds of fairy penguins waddle up the beach to the safety of their burrows in the sand dunes. You can watch this magical procession from viewing stands and boardwalks. The penguins visit all year round, though their numbers peak from October to January when as many as 1000 come ashore every evening. Phillip Island is a scenic 90-minute drive from Melbourne; plan to arrive an hour before sunset.

For further information visit www.penguins.org.au

ISLANDS

Papua New Guinea

39 Tari

In the Southern Highlands, Tari Valley and the mountains above it are some of the best places for bird-watching in all New Guinea, especially for birds of paradise. The Huli people who live in this valley are also amongst the most traditional in the country – the men still build fabulous wigs of human hair topped with the feathers of birds of paradise, parrots and eagles. Ambua Lodge, nestled at 2000 m (6500 feet) in beautiful southern beech forests, is an ideal place from which to explore the area.

For further information visit www.pngtours.com

40 Sepik River

The Sepik's floodplain is a vast area of swamps, lakes and waterways, bordered by steep, forest-covered hills. Options for exploring it range from hiring a local canoe from Ambunti to expensive cruises on luxury boats and an exclusive lodge on a small tributary at Karawari. The waterlily- and lotus-covered lakes are home to whistling ducks, pygmy geese and a variety of other water birds, as well as saltwater crocodiles. The forested banks are a great place to look for spotted cuscus and a variety of birds of paradise, including the 12 wired species. This region is also famous for its traditional carvings and magnificent spirit houses.

41 Madang

This small town on the north coast is protected by a barrier reef enclosing a large lagoon which is

PAPUA NEW GUINEA

Port Moresby

excellent for diving. In the forest nearby there are also many caves and sinkholes, home to numerous species of bats. The town itself has a large camp of spectacled flying foxes which fly out at dusk, providing a wonderful wildlife spectacle.

42 Lae

The Rainforest Habitat at the university in Lae has the most complete collection of New Guinea's mammals, birds, reptiles and insects. Most are housed in an impressive walk-through enclosure planted with rainforest trees.

43 Rabaul, New Britain

Surrounded by active volcanoes, this is the biggest town on the island. The old town was largely destroyed by an eruption in 1994 and a new one is being built further away from the volcanoes. Tuvurvur volcano is still smoking and can be viewed from the road or by a boat trip in the bay to land on its shores. It's not possible to climb Tuvurvur because of the poisonous gases it emits, but a short helicopter flight around the summit gives fabulous views into the crater. At its base there are numerous holes dug by megapode birds, which use the warm volcanic soil to incubate their eggs.

44 Kimbe Bay, New Britain

This bay is ringed with volcanoes and has some of the prettiest coral reefs anywhere. These can be dived from Walindi Plantation Resort, which at one time or another has provided a base for most of the world's best underwater photographers. The great attraction here is the overwhelming variety of marine life, although the forests nearby have volcanic hot springs and even a hot river you can swim in, as well as more megapodes.

For further information about diving in Kimbe Bay visit www.walindi.com and for diving throughout Papua New Guinea visit the PNG Divers Association site at www.pngdive.com

It is difficult to generalize about the best time to visit New Guinea. December to March is generally considered the wet season and May to October the dry, but this is highly variable and even reversed in some locations. You can experience fabulous weather any time of year so there is certainly no off-season.

For information about travel throughout PNG visit www.pngtourism.org.pg or www.geocities.com/skyfdn/PNGlinks

45 Lord Howe Island

This is part of Australia and just a short flight from either Sydney or Brisbane. It's an idyllic spot for nature lovers with 14 species of nesting sea birds; bracing cliff-top walks to view the aerial acrobatics of tropic birds and sooty terns; an exhilarating hike up through the forests of Mount Gower; or diving and snorkelling on the coral, which forms the world's most southerly reef.

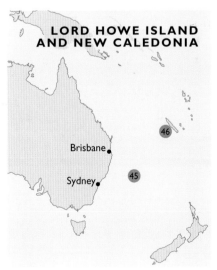

LORD HOWE ISLAND AND NEW CALEDONIA

Brisbane

Sydney

Visitor numbers are restricted, so it's important to book in advance; most people travel around this small island on foot or on bicycles, which can be hired locally. Spring and early summer are the best times for viewing breeding sea birds.

For further information visit www.lordhoweisland.info

46 New Caledonia

New Caledonia has been politically a part of France for the last 150 years. Its most impressive natural feature is the enormous barrier reef, which makes for excellent diving and snorkelling all year round. Although much of the forest has been felled, there are still good examples of its unusual native vegetation. Ile de Pins, off the southern tip, has beautiful araucaria trees lining its fabulous beaches. Parc de la Rivière Bleue offers the best opportunity to see New Caledonia's rare and unique national bird, the cagou, as well as walks through beautiful native forest.

For further information visit www.newcaledoniatourism-south.com

New Zealand

47 Banks Peninsula, South Island

This is *the* place to come if you want to watch, or even swim with, the world's smallest dolphin, the Hector's, which is unique to New Zealand. Trips run out of Akaroa and Lyttelton and summer is the most pleasant time to visit. The peninsula is also a stronghold for the blue penguin.

Further information from www.akaroa.com for Akaroa and lyttinfo@ihug.co.nz for Lyttelton.

48 Kaikoura, South Island

This is one of the world's best locations for watching marine mammals. There are daily boat trips to locate sperm whales and to watch or swim with dusky dolphins. You can snorkel with New Zealand fur seals and undertake cage dives to view sharks. This is also a hotspot for sea birds, including several species of albatross. You can visit all year round although sea conditions are more pleasant in summer.

For further information visit www.dolphin.co.nz, www.whalewatch.co.nz and www.kaikoura.co.nz

49 Queenstown, South Island

The ski resorts around Queenstown are home to keas, the world's only alpine parrots. Gangs of them raid the cafés for leftover food and provide a very comical sight playing in the snow. Other good spots to look out for them are at the Homer Tunnel on the road to Milford Sound and at Arthur's Pass National Park.

For further information on Queenstown visit www.queenstown-nz.co.nz

50 Otago Peninsula, South Island

A short drive outside Dunedin, Taiaroa Head on the Otago Peninsula is a great place to see nesting royal albatross, New Zealand sea lions sleeping on the beach and yellow-eyed penguins returning to their burrows in the evening. You can visit Otago Peninsula any time of year but the albatross colony is closed during the breeding season, from mid-September to late November. However, even then you can observe the birds from the visitor centre via a remote camera.

For further information visit www.dunedintourism.co.nz

51 Rotorua, North Island

This small town rivals even Yellowstone in America for its diversity of geothermal features such as hot springs, bubbling mud pools and spectacular geysers. Right in the heart of town, Whakarewarewa is one of the most varied. There are even hot springs directly beneath the houses. Wai-O-Tapu has a large geyser, bubbling mud pools and coloured geothermal terraces. The walk at Waimangu meanders through beautiful forest and a series of geysers and steaming pools down to Lake Rotomahana, where a boat trip

1

gives good views of Mount Tarawera, which blew up in a devastating eruption in 1886, killing over 100 people.

For further information visit www.rotoruanz.com

Offshore Islands

New Zealand has many offshore island wildlife sanctuaries, but most are closed to the public or accessible only with special permits. Good bird islands that can be visited with a special permit include Little Barrier (in the Hauraki Gulf, near Auckland) 52 and Kapiti (off the west coast, north of Wellington) 53 . However, Tiritiri Matangi Island 54 is open to the public and is a great place to see unique New Zealand birds as it's only a short ferry trip from Auckland. Many species of birds have been introduced to the island to establish breeding populations and now it's home to tuis, bellbirds, fantails, takahe, saddlebacks, little spotted kiwi, whiteheads, parakeets, robins, brown teal and blue penguins.

Further information on New Zealand wildlife can be found by visiting the Department of Conservation site www.doc.govt.nz, for birds www.forest-bird.org.nz and for travel www.purenz.com

1. Pohutu Geyser in Whakarewarewa, Rotorua, North Island, New Zealand

2. Two Peoples Bay, Western Australia

NEW WORLDS

55 Royal Botanic Gardens, Melbourne

One of the world's finest botanic gardens, established more than 150 years ago, the Royal Botanic Gardens are an oasis in the middle of the city. There is a huge range of plant collections and a large lake with black swans, but one of the more spectacular sights is the colony of large grey-headed flying foxes that has taken up residence in an area called Fern Gully. It's the most southerly colony of fruit bats in the world and it's quite something to see them at such close quarters above the rose garden. It is worth waiting until dusk to see them head out to feed – watch from one of the nearby bridges as they fly over the Yarra River, past the skyscrapers and neon lights. They are damaging the trees where they roost and there are controversial plans to reduce their numbers.

For information on the botanic gardens visit www.rbgmelb.org.au

56 Fitzroy Gardens, Melbourne

For night-time city wildlife-watchers, Melbourne's big parks are good places to visit. Here you will probably come across brush-tail possums so used to urban life that they raid dustbins after dark and allow people to feed them with fruit. Try Fitzroy Gardens in East Melbourne. It's probably the easiest way to see one of Australia's most familiar animals.

57 Anglesea Golf Club, Victoria

It's a strange sight to see kangaroos grazing on the fairway and sitting around the sprinklers as people play golf around them, but that is what happens at Anglesea Golf Club, about a two-hour drive southwest of Melbourne. There are hundreds of resident grey kangaroos here and they are quite a tourist attraction. Galahs – pink and grey parrots – are also common around the course and are fun to watch. Anglesea itself is the start of the Great Ocean Road, a stunning drive along Victoria's southwest coastline.

58 Sydney Harbour

Sydney must be one of the few major cities in the world with a national park at its heart. There are beautiful walks through native vegetation beside the water, with plenty of birdlife and magnificent views of the city, in Sydney Harbour National Park. The Royal Botanic Gardens, between the harbour and the central business district, are great for bird-watching, too, with over 100 species being recorded, and they also have a large

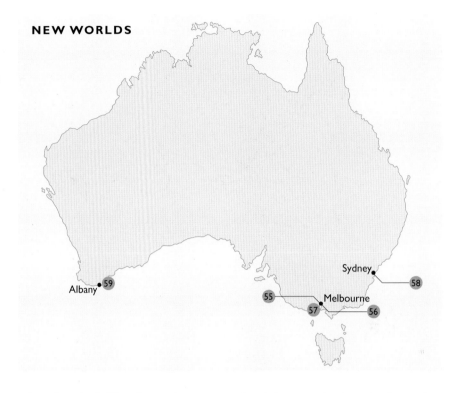

NEW WORLDS

colony of grey-headed flying foxes. In the harbour itself marine mammals are occasionally spotted; recently a right whale and calf spent several days amongst the busy boat traffic in the heart of the city, under the Harbour Bridge.

For further information on the national park visit www.nationalparks.nsw.gov.au and for the botanic gardens www.rbgsyd.gov.au

59 Two Peoples Bay, Western Australia

This is a place to come to look for rarities: there have been several recent remarkable 'rediscoveries' of animals thought to be extinct. Gilbert's potoroo was found here only a few years ago,

though there are so few that seeing them in the wild is unlikely. But you may well hear the loud call of the noisy scrub-bird, another 'lost-and-found' animal and still very rare. In any case, there are plenty of other birds here, including many sea birds. Kangaroos bound around and southern right whales pass along the coast in winter. It is worth visiting just for the scenery, with its flowery heathlands and beautiful shoreline. The bay is a short drive from the nearest town, Albany, on the southwest corner of Western Australia.

For further information visit www.calm.wa.gov.au/national_parks

Acknowledgements

During the making of the television series on which this book is based we travelled throughout Australasia and were introduced to intriguing stories, wonderful locations and spectacular wildlife by a whole range of scientists, naturalists, land owners, rangers and others who have dedicated their lives to investigating and protecting the natural wonders in this region. They generously gave us a privileged understanding of the natural history of Australasia for which we are extremely grateful and without which this book would not have been possible. They include Michael Baratt, Paul Barker, Peter Bartlett, Pam Bates, Lars Bejder, Max and Cecilie Benjamin, Paddy Berry, Terry Carmichael, Rita Cattoni, Dean Ah Chee, Peter Clarke, Peter Comber, Bill and Wendy Cooper, Christine Crafter, Chris Day, Chris Dickman, Pearce Doherty, Birgit Dorges, Dale Eglitis, Tim Flannery, Tony Friend, Gary Fry, George Gibbs, Cindy Nagamarra Gibson, Mitjili Napananga Gibson, Malcolm Gill, Mike Gillam, Karen Gowlett-Holmes, Steve Hamilton, Jurgen Heucke, Paul Jansen, Richard Kingsford, Lars Kogge, Vilia Lawrence, Phillip Leahy, Murray Logan, Richard Loyn, Louise Marsh, Dennis Matthews, Karen May, Keith McDonald, Don Merton, Ian Morris, Rod Morris, Rex Niendorf, Graham Phelps, Simon Plowright, Bob Prior, Tanya Rankin, Julian Reid, Don Rowlands, Craig and Jessie Shankland, Allen Sheather, Ann Thresher, KeithWard, Mary White, Tony Whitaker and John Woinarski.

We shared our exploration of Australasia with dedicated wildlife camera crews, who not only captured fabulous film sequences and photographs but were also great travelling companions. We are very grateful to Barrie Britton, Peter Coleman, Lindsay and Ruth Cupper, Leighton De Barros, Pieter de Vries, Roger Dundas, Wade Fairley, Richard Fitzpatrick, Kevin Flay, Bryce Grunden, David Hannan, Nick Hayward, Mark Lamble, Mike Lemmon, Rory McGuinness, Peter Nearhos, Andrew Penniket, Mike Pitts, Damon Smith, Gavin Thurston, Aldo Valastro and Peter Zakharov.

In our research, travel and filming we were supported by wonderful production teams, based in the ABC Natural History Unit in Melbourne and the BBC Natural History Unit in Bristol. Our very special thanks go to Martin Cohen, Amanda Ford, Dione Gilmour, Laura Harvey, Robert Hayward, Clare Huey, Luke Hunter, Christine Lipari, Josie Matthiesson, Clare Thomson, Di Williams and Simon Williams. We are also very grateful to Tim Flannery, director of the South Australian Museum and one of Australia's most inspiring biological scientists, for taking the time to write an excellent foreword.

For their enthusiasm, encouragement and the production flair that has created such a beautiful book we would also like to thank Frances Abraham, Shirley Patton, Lisa Pettibone, Martin Redfern, Nicky Ross and Caroline Taggart at BBC Books.

Bibliography

Andrew N., *Under Southern Seas – The Ecology of Australia's Rocky Reefs* (UNSW Press, 1999).

Archer M., Hand S. and Godthelp H., *Australia's Lost World* (New Holland Publishers, 2000).

Bauer A. and Sadlier R., *The Herpetofauna of New Caledonia* (Society for the Study of Amphibians and Reptiles, 2000).

Beehler B., Pratt T. and Zimmerman D., *Birds of New Guinea* (Princeton University Press, 1986).

Bennett J. et al, *Watching Wildlife Australia* (Lonely Planet Publications, 2000).

Bonaccorso F., *Bats of Papua New Guinea* (Conservation International, 1998).

Bradman F., Arnold B. and Bell S. (eds), *A Natural History of the Lake Eyre Region: A Visitor's Guide* (South Australia National Parks & Wildlife Service, 1991).

Breeden S., *Australian World Heritage Tropical Rainforest* (Steve Parish Publishing).

Breeden S., *Uluru: Looking after Uluru–Kata Tjuta the Anangu Way* (J. B. Books, 1997).

Coates B., *The Birds of Papua New Guinea*, Vols I and II (Dove Publications, 1985 and 1990).

Cogger H., *Reptiles and Amphibians of Australia* (New Holland Publishers, 2000).

Coleman N. and Marsh N., *Diving Australia. A Guide to the Best Diving Down Under* (Periplus Editions, 1997).

Corbett L., *The Dingo in Australia and Asia* (J.B. Books, 2001).

Dawson T., *Kangaroos: Biology of the Largest Marsupials* (UNSW Press, 1995).

Diamond J. and Bond A., *Kea, Bird of Paradox* (University of California Press, 1999).

Eldridge S. and Reid J., *A Biological Survey of the Finke Floodout Region, Northern Territory* (ALEC and Australian Heritage Commission, 2000).

Flannery T., *Mammals of New Guinea* (Robert Brown and Associates, 1990).

Flannery T., *The Future Eaters* (Reed Books, 1994).

Flannery T., Martin R. and Szalay A., *Tree Kangaroos, A Curious Natural History* (Reed Books, 1996).

Fox A., *The National Parks and Other Wild Places of Australia* (New Holland, 2001).

Gibbs G., *New Zealand Weta* (Reed Books, 1998).

Gill P. and Burke C., *Whale Watching in Australian and New Zealand Waters* (New Holland Publishers, 1999).

Gill P. and Burke C., *Whale Watching* (New Holland Publishers, 1999).

Grant T., *The Platypus, a Unique Mammal* (UNSW Press, 1995).

Greig D., *Field Guide to Australian Wild Flowers* (New Holland, 1999).

Hall L. and Richards G., *Flying Foxes, Fruit and Blossom Bats of Australia* (UNSW Press, 2000).

Haynes R., *Seeking the Centre: The Australian Desert in Literature, Art and Film* (Cambridge University Press, 1998).

Hoatson D. et al, *Bungle Bungle Range* (Australian Geological Survey Organization, 1997).

Hoatson D. et al, *Kakadu and Nitmiluk* (Australian Geological Organization, 2000).

Hutching G., *The Natural World of New Zealand* (Penguin Books NZ Ltd, 1998).

Hutton I., *The Australian Geographic Book of Lord Howe Island* (Australian Geographic, 1998).

Kerle A., *Possums, the Brushtails, Ringtails and Greater Glider* (UNSW Press, 2001).

Latz P., *Bushfires and Bushtucker: Aboriginal Plant Use in Central Australia* (IAD Press, 1995).

Low T., *Feral Future* (Viking, 1999).

Low T., *The New Nature* (Viking, 2002).

Menkhorst P. and Knight F., *A Field Guide to Mammals of Australia* (Oxford University Press, 2001).

Menzies J., *A Handbook of New Guinea Marsupials & Monotremes* (Kristen Press Inc, 1991).

Moon G., *New Zealand, Offshore Islands and their Wildlife* (Reed Books, 1995).

Morris I., *Kakadu National Park, Australia* (Steve Parish Publishing).

Morton S. and Mulvaney D. (eds), *Exploring Central Australia: Society, the Environment and the 1894 Horn Expedition* (Surrey Beatty & Sons, 1996).

Moyal A., *Platypus* (Allen & Unwin, 2001).

Nielsen L., *Daintree, Jewel of Tropical North Queensland* (Lloyd Nielsen, 1997).

Nightingale N., *New Guinea* (BBC Books, 1992).

Ombler K., *The National Parks and Other Wild Places of New Zealand* (New Holland, 2001).

Oosterzee P. van, *The Centre: The Natural History of Australia's Desert Regions* (Reed Books, 1991).

Pizzey G. and Knight F., *Field Guide to the Birds of Australia* (Angus and Robertson, 1997).

Queensland Museum, *Wildlife of Tropical North Queensland* (Queensland Museum, 2000).

Read I., *The Bush, A Guide to the Vegetated Landscapes of Australia* (UNSW Press, 1994).

Reader's Digest, *Encyclopedia of Australian Wildlife* (Reader's Digest, 1997).

Rismiller P., *The Echidna, Australia's Enigma* (Hugh Lauter Levin Associates, Inc, 1999).

Rolls E., *Australia, A Biography* (University of Queensland Press, 2000).

Rolls E., *They All Ran Wild* (Angus and Robertson, 1969).

Ryan P. and Paulin C., *Fiordland Underwater, New Zealand's Hidden Wilderness* (Exisle Publishing, 1998).

Serventy V., *The Desert Sea: The Miracle of Lake Eyre in Flood* (Macmillan, 1985).

Shepherd M., *The Simpson Desert: Natural History and Human Endeavour* (Reed Books, 1994).

Simpson K. and Wilson Z., *Birdwatching In Australia and New Zealand* (Reed New Holland, 1998).

Simpson K. and Day N., *Field Guide to the Birds of Australia* (Viking, 1996).

Stanton J. & Skipsey B., *The Australian Geographic Book of the Red Centre* (Australian Geographic, 1995).

Strahan R. (ed.), *The Mammals of Australia* (Reed New Holland, 2000).

Sturman A. and Tapper N., *The Weather and Climate of Australia and New Zealand* (Oxford University Press, 1996).

Sutherland S. and Nolch G., *Dangerous Australian Animals* (Hyland House, 2000).

Temple P., *The Book of the Kea* (Hodder Moa Beckett Publishers, 1996).

Thompson R., *A Guide to the Geology and Landforms of Central Australia* (Northern Territory Dept Mines and Energy, 1995).

Triggs B., *The Wombat, Common Wombats in Australia* (UNSW Press, 1996).

Vincent M. and Wilson S., *Australian Goannas* (New Holland, 1999).

Wager R. & Ulmack P., *Fishes of the Lake Eyre Catchment of Central Australia* (Dept of Primary Industries & Qld Fisheries Service, 2000).

Watts D., *Tasmanian Mammals, A Field Guide* (Peregrine Press, 1993).

Webb G. and Manolis C., *Crocodiles of Australia* (Reed New Holland, 1998).

White M., *After the Greening, The Browning of Australia* (Kangaroo Press, 1998).

White M., *Listen … Our Land is Crying* (Kangaroo Press, 1997).

White M., *Running Down, Water in a Changing Land* (Kangaroo Press, 2000).

White M., *The Greening of Gondwana* (Kangaroo Press, 1998).

Williams J. and Woinarski J., *Eucalypt Ecology* (Cambridge University Press, 1997).

Woodford J., *The Wollemi Pine* (Text Publishing, 2000).

Zborowski P. and Storey R., *A Field Guide to Insects in Australia* (Reed New Holland, 1998).

Zeidler W. and Ponder W. (eds), *Natural History of Dalhousie Springs* (South Australian Museum, 1989).

Zell L., *Diving and Snorkelling Australia's Great Barrier Reef* (Lonely Planet Publications, 1999).

BBC Worldwide would like to thank the following for providing photographs and for permission to reproduce copyright material. While every effort has been made to trace and acknowledge all copyright holders, we would like to apologize should there have been any errors or omissions.

Index